the simple guide to Marine AQUARIUMS

Jeffrey Kurtz

Maroon Clownfish.

T.F.H. Publications, Inc.

© 2002 T.F.H. Publications, Inc.

Distributed in the UNITED STATES to the Pet Trade by T.F.H. Publications, Inc., 1 TFH Plaza, Neptune City, NJ 07753; on the Internet at www.tfh.com; in CANADA by Rolf C. Hagen Inc., 3225 Sartelon St., Montreal, Quebec H4R 1E8; Pet Trade by H & L Pet Supplies Inc., 27 Kingston Crescent, Kitchener, Ontario N2B 2T6; in ENGLAND by T.F.H. Publications, PO Box 74, Havant PO9 5TT; in AUSTRALIA AND THE SOUTH PACIFIC by T.F.H. (Australia), Pty. Ltd., Box 149, Brookvale 2100 N.S.W., Australia; in NEW ZEALAND by Brooklands Aquarium Ltd., 5 McGiven Drive, New Plymouth, RD1 New Zealand; in SOUTH AFRICA by Rolf C. Hagen S.A. (PTY.) LTD., P.O. Box 201199, Durban North 4016, South Africa; in Japan by T.F.H. Publications. Published by T.F.H. Publications, Inc.

Manufactured in the United States of America by T.F.H. Publications, Inc.

Contents

Bacteria:
The Good
Kind

pH:
Keep it up!

Trouble:
Avoid it!

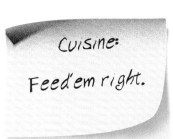

Cuisine:

Feed'em right.

Part One
Getting into Marines

"Junior! Get out of those bubbles! You don't know where they've been!"

Thinking of Taking the Plunge into Salt Water?

Starting a marine aquarium is one of those under-takings that many people contemplate on and off for years before actually "taking the plunge." Some hesitate because they feel overwhelmed by all of the high-tech-sounding gadgets and scientific terminology associated with the saltwater hobby. Others may find the relatively high cost of certain marine specimens and the equipment needed to properly maintain them to be prohibitive. Then there are those once-bitten-twice-shy individuals who are afraid to start another marine tank after trying once and failing. While each of these concerns has some validity, it would be a shame to allow them to become impediments to success in the marine aquarium hobby.

The water's fine and I'm glad to meet you.

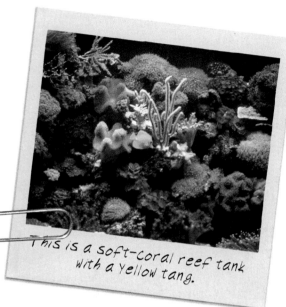

This is a soft-coral reef tank with a yellow tang.

There's no question that equipment plays an important role in maintaining a healthy marine aquarium, and many aquarists do take a shine to high-tech gadgets. You could also argue that much of the marine aquarium literature available today is long on technical jargon and short on clear, concise information written specifically for the beginner. But the truth of the matter is, regardless of your background or the size of your pocketbook, you can enjoy a thriving marine microcosm at home using only a minimum of equipment–and you won't need a doctorate in marine biology or chemistry to achieve it!

Throughout the pages of this book, I'll attempt to clarify the most important technical aspects of setting up and maintaining a marine fish-only or mini-reef aquarium without burying you in a lot of scientific blather. I believe that the simplest explanation is usually the best explanation, and also I'm just not all that scientific-minded myself. Along with the technical stuff, we'll take a look at lots of "fintastic" facts and interesting anecdotes about the various creatures that inhabit the world's oceans. So with no further ado, let's get ready to "get our feet wet" in the fascinating world of the marine aquarium.

What are the benefits of a saltwater aquarium?

Marine aquariums offer numerous advantages to those who maintain them. Of course, there's the simple satisfaction of creating a beautiful ocean ecosystem within the confines of five glass (or acrylic) panes–an achievement to be proud of when you consider the delicate balance of life that exists on the natural coral reefs. From a purely esthetic angle, you'd be hard pressed to find anything more captivating in the home.

Zanclus cornutus, the Moorish Idol, is a delicate fish that rarely survives in the aquarium.

What other decorative element can compare to the spectacular drama that is played out every day in a community of marine fish or the dazzling interplay of light, color, and hypnotic motion in the mini-reef aquarium?

Making a splash in the classroom

Apart from its obvious beauty, the marine aquarium is also an excellent educational tool. While the closed system of the aquarium is not technically a natural environment, it is still the best way, without actually donning SCUBA gear, to teach children and adults alike about the interconnectedness of the coral reef ecosystem and the hazards of neglecting or abusing it. As an instructional tool in the high school or elementary classroom, the marine aquarium is unrivaled, especially when the students are encouraged to be directly involved in all aspects of setup and maintenance–cycling, testing water parameters, selecting compatible specimens, treating ailments, water changes, and so on–rather than just feeding the fish.

Of course, the educational opportunities provided by the marine aquarium don't stop at the classroom. Why not get the whole family involved in setting up a home aquarium, using the same educational approach? Assign age-appropriate duties to each child (and, of course, your spouse if he or she is willing), and try to link each maintenance task to its counterpart in nature. For example, give your kindergartner the responsibility of turning the aquarium lights on at the same time each day, and explain how the lighting system takes the place of the sun. Let an older child empty the protein skimmer's waste-collecting cup, and draw a correlation between protein skimming and the effects of wind and waves on a body of water.

Conservation and the marine aquarium

In many ways, marine aquarium hobbyists are in the best position to promote the conservation of the world's coral reefs. After all, the first step toward preserving an endangered habitat is to develop an understanding of–and a love for– the organisms that exist within it. While the role of the scientific community in marine

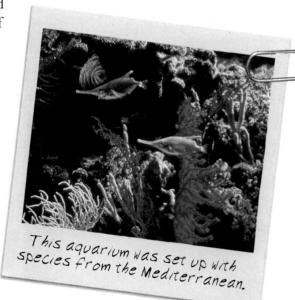

This aquarium was set up with species from the Mediterranean.

Food fit for marine fry

In the not-so-distant past, one of the biggest obstacles to successfully rearing the fry of marine fish was finding a live food source small enough to fit into their tiny mouths. After hatching, the young of many marine fish species spend several days to several weeks drifting in the water column among the plankton. There they can choose from a wide variety of tiny prey items and feast to their hearts' content. However, this is not the case within the confines of the aquarium, where food must be provided by the aquarist.

Commercial and amateur breeders alike have since found that perfect first food in the marine rotifer—a miniscule multi-cellular organism, about one-third the size of a newly hatched brine shrimp, which is extremely resilient and easy to culture.

But there's an amusing twist. Aquarists who wish to culture marine rotifers must also develop a culture of a particular single-celled alga (so-called green water) in order to feed the rotifers—a food to feed the food to feed the fry. Marine rotifers are available along with the algae they feed on in starter cultures through many aquarium supply companies.

conservation is undeniable, it is often the private hobbyist who first observes unique behaviors that may have significant survival value for a particular fish or invertebrate species.

Take breeding, for example. It was once a widely held belief that getting marine fish species to successfully reproduce in captivity was next to impossible. Even if a captive-spawning event did occur, it was commonly assumed that raising the young to adulthood was simply not a viable proposition. This was attributed to two important characteristics held in common by the young of many marine fish species. One is that they have a prolonged pelagic stage during which they drift freely with the plankton rafts in the open ocean–a stage that can be very difficult to recreate in a closed aquarium system. The other is that they demand a steady supply of miniscule plankton as their first food–a daunting challenge for all but the most dedicated aquarist. But in spite of the gloomy odds, some amateur hobbyists have risen to the challenge and developed techniques for successfully breeding and rearing certain marine species. This happens sometimes by accident and sometimes through repeated painstaking experiments on the aquarists' part. Also, a staggering amount has been learned about the behavior, care requirements, defense mechanisms, and reproductive strategies of corals and other sessile (immobile) invertebrates by observing them over long periods of time in the aquarium setting.

A saltwater stress reliever

Another important role played by the marine aquarium is that of "pressure-relief valve." When the tensions of career, family, and the world at large combine to create an overwhelming wave of anxiety, a few minutes in front of a well-maintained aquarium will help to restore your tranquility and sense of well-being. Of course, the emphasis in the preceding statement must be placed on the "well-maintained" part. If you've chosen an assortment of peaceful, compatible species and carefully provided for their different nutritional and environmental needs, your marine tank will, indeed, be a source of pleasure as well as an outlet for life's little anxieties. On the other hand, an aquarium that is out of balance in some way–that is, the fish are in poor health or constantly "at each other's throats," or the corals and other invertebrates are mysteriously dying off–will quickly become a source of stress rather than a sanctuary from it.

The blue trigger, Pseudobalistes fuscus.

The marine aquarium and the novice aquarist

If you've never kept an aquarium of any kind before, you may be saying to yourself, "Maybe I'd be better off if I started with a freshwater aquarium before attempting a marine tank. After all, they're supposed to be much easier, right?" Well you probably could make a convincing argument that many freshwater setups are easier and more goof-proof than most marine aquariums. However, you could also make the argument that some freshwater setups are just as complicated (if not more so) as a basic marine setup.

Modern equipment favors success for beginners

The early days of marine fishkeeping were a logistical and technical nightmare for even the most seasoned aquarists, let alone for newcomers to the hobby. For one thing, there were no commercially manufactured artificial salt mixes to speak of. Hobbyists either had to create their own, using haphazard recipes, or make frequent trips to the shore to collect natural salt water, which likely contained a vast array of pollutants and pathogenic organisms. At the same time, very little filtration, lighting, and heating equipment was

Go ahead! Dive right in!

As with the marine aquarium hobby, modern technology has made it much easier for the fish fanatic to get an up-close-and-personal view of life on the coral reef as a SCUBA diver. What was once an activity reserved only for the fittest adventurer or outdoor enthusiast can now be enjoyed by almost anyone, including your average "couch potato."

While SCUBA has always been an equipment-intensive sport, it wasn't until the 1980s that the manufacturers of SCUBA equipment began to tailor their products to meet the specific needs and capabilities of the casual diver. Now SCUBA diving has become considerably safer as well as more "democratic." With the advent of high-tech buoyancy compensators, low-cost and user-friendly dive computers, high-performance regulators, and ergonomically designed fins, men and women of all ages and fitness levels can experience the world beneath the waves.

If you've been wondering what it would be like to "get in the swim" so you can see some of those fascinating marine organisms firsthand, now may be the perfect time to give SCUBA a try. After all, why should the athletic types have all the fun?

being manufactured specifically for the marine aquarium, and any products that were designed for use in salt water tended to be outrageously expensive. In addition, very little was known about the care requirements of most marine fish, so keeping them alive was a hit-or-miss prospect at best.

Today several factors favor success for the first-time aquarist, including the availability of high-quality synthetic salt mixes, a vast array of modern "life-support" equipment manufactured specifically for the marine aquarium, and, of course, the wealth of information and literature about the marine aquarium hobby that has been accumulated through years of trial and error.

Starting with the mini-reef: putting the cart before the horse?

We've more or less established that there's no compelling reason for first-time aquarists to start out with a freshwater tank as a sort of apprenticeship toward salt water. But what about setting up a mini-reef right off the starting block? Can a novice hobbyist succeed with a mini-reef–arguably the pinnacle of achievement in the world of marine aquariums–without first gaining experience with a fish-only tank?

Before answering that question, it might be helpful to explain what the actual difference is between a fish-only tank and a mini-reef. The fish-only tank is fairly self-explanatory. It's basically an aquarium housing either a community of compatible marine fish or a tank with a single specimen that is best kept alone due to its large size, aggressiveness, or predatory nature. Certain benign crustaceans and mollusks may also be included in the fish-only setup (at least as I interpret it), although this may seem to be contradictory. The mini-reef, on the other hand, focuses mostly on various hard and soft corals, sponges, anemones, and other sessile invertebrates, many of which demand special high-intensity lighting for survival. If fish and motile invertebrates are included in the mini-reef at all, they will be few in number and inoffensive toward the sessile invertebrates. Because fish waste and uneaten fish food tend to degrade water quality, some mini-reef aquarists choose not to include fish at all.

Anyway, the answer to the question posed earlier is a very tentative "yes." If you're willing to invest the time for research and you have the patience to take things one step at a time with no shortcuts, you'll probably do okay starting out with a mini-reef. However, I would have to add the following caveat: mini-reef aquariums demand absolutely impeccable water quality at all times, and fluctuating water conditions can spell disaster for your valued invertebrate specimens. Considering the fact that learning to control water parameters takes a little experimentation by most new aquarists, it's probably a good idea to gradually

Aquarium research in the information age

With the advent of the Internet, budding marine aquarists can have instant access to a staggering number of research sources with just a few simple keystrokes. Many aquarium-related websites provide very useful information for the beginner and expert alike, and some of the chat rooms are great places to go to get immediate feedback and insights from fellow aquarists.

On the other hand, some of the information circulating out there in cyberspace about marine aquariums is largely unsubstantiated or contradictory and must be taken with a grain of salt (excuse the pun). Remember, there are no Internet editors out there to separate the wheat from the chaff, so to speak, and there is no software that can filter out dubious or misleading claims.

So how can you be sure you're getting the straight story on the Web? First, consider the source. Have you seen other written materials by the author in aquarium magazines, books, or newsletters? Secondly, look for redundancy. Does the information or claim jibe with what you've read on other Web pages and in other sources? Finally, apply a little common sense. If the information strikes you as being beyond the pale, it probably is.

build up to the mini-reef as your experience and confidence grow. After all, you don't want your first foray into the world of the marine aquarium to end in frustration and disillusionment.

When freshwater aquarists go marine

Experienced freshwater aficionados who would like to have a go at keeping a saltwater aquarium will find that making the switch is relatively easy. In fact, most of the important principles that pertain to freshwater aquariums also apply to marine tanks. The process of cycling the aquarium is exactly the same. Proper stocking and feeding rates are just as important. The three basic forms of filtration–mechanical, chemical, and biological–still apply. Water changes are still the cornerstone of water quality maintenance. And, with a few notable exceptions, most of the necessary equipment can be carried over from fresh water to salt water as well.

"Sticker shock"

One important distinction freshwater hobbyists will observe almost immediately is the relatively high cost of certain marine specimens when compared to the cost of the freshwater fish they're used to buying. I can still recall my first trip to a saltwater dealer to buy fish for my debut marine tank. I had been keeping freshwater tanks on and off for many years and was accustomed to forking over no more than a dollar or two for the various tetras, livebearers, and barbs that typically inhabited my tanks. Needless to say, when the total

Making the switch from fresh to salt water?

Items that carry over	Items to purchase
All-glass or acrylic tank	High-intensity fluorescent or metal halide lighting (mini-reef only)
Wooden or acrylic stand	
Newer submersible heater(s)	Protein skimmer
Floating or fixed thermometer(s)	Reverse osmosis water purifier
Standard fluorescent lights (fish-only)	High-quality sea salt mix
	Hydrometer
Canister, hang-on-tank, undergravel filters (replace filter media)	Crushed coral or aragonite substrate and rockwork
Wet/dry filter system (replace filter media)	Ammonia, nitrite, nitrate, and pH test kits for saltwater tanks
Siphon, brushes, tongs, algae magnet, nets, etc.	Calcium and trace element supplements (mini-reef only)
	UV sterilizer (optional)
Power heads (must be safe for salt water)	

*All used equipment must be thoroughly rinsed before transfer to new aquarium.

was rung up for my new marine specimens, my chin almost hit the floor. I also recall thinking at the time that the pressure was really on to keep those poor things alive. After all, it's one thing to lose a 99¢ neon tetra, but losing a $30 regal tang is another matter altogether.

So why the high cost? For one thing, most marine fish are still hand-collected in the wild. If you've ever attempted to keep pace with a frightened reef fish while diving or snorkeling, you can imagine how labor intensive and time consuming it is to actually net those little swifties. (Of course, some collectors use poisons and other destructive practices to make capture easier, but that's a topic for another chapter.) The high price tag can also be attributed to the high mortality rate during shipping and handling. With so many specimens coming all the way from the tropical Pacific and Indian Oceans (often kept in the same bag and in the same dirty water throughout the long journey), it's not surprising that many perish in transit.

Always try to select captive-bred marine fish and invertebrates.

Captive-bred fish: Are they worth the price?

Considering the fact that captive-bred marine fish tend to cost substantially more than their wild-caught counterparts, you might ask yourself whether captive-bred specimens are really worth the higher price tag. The answer is an emphatic yes! Marine fish bred in captivity offer several advantages to aquarists, even though they may present no visible characteristics to distinguish them from wild-caught specimens.

Since captive-bred fish do not endure the stress of capture and prolonged transportation, their survival rate in the aquarium is much higher. They've also learned to accept such standard aquarium fare as flake, pellet, and freeze-dried foods, which means you're less likely to be faced with a "hunger strike." In addition, buying captive-bred specimens takes some of the collecting pressure off the natural coral reefs, which are in decline in many parts of the world.

So what about the higher cost? Considering the ease with which captive-bred fish acclimate to aquarium conditions and the fact that they have a lower mortality rate than wild-caught specimens, you may actually end up paying less in the long run. After all, an inexpensive fish that dies shortly after purchase is really no bargain at all.

Part 1

By contrast, many popular freshwater species are commercially captive-bred in large numbers, which helps to keep their cost down. Besides, some freshwater fish breed so readily in captivity and are so easy to rear (e.g., the livebearers: platies, guppies, swordtails, and mollies) that a small investment for a breeding pair yields more offspring than the average aquarist can handle. On a positive note for marine aquarists, captive breeding of certain saltwater fish is becoming more and more commercially viable, and the cost of captive-bred specimens is gradually coming down as technical advances are made in these programs.

"Bread-and-butter" beauties

In spite of their higher price tag, some of the more beautiful marine fish are surprisingly hardy and forgiving in captivity. The brilliantly colored clownfish (*Amphiprion ocellaris*) comes to mind, as does the stunning coral beauty (*Centropyge bispinosus*), and the wildly patterned Picasso trigger (*Rhinecanthus aculeatus*). Not only are all of these fish strikingly attractive, but they are also amazingly resilient, which makes them ideal choices for the beginner. This stands in stark contrast to the freshwater side of the hobby, where it seems as if the more attractive a fish is, the more delicate and temperamental it is, and therefore the more difficult it is for a beginner to keep. Of course, as they say, beauty is in the eye of the beholder, and many freshwater enthusiasts would challenge my less-than-objective appraisal of the attractiveness of freshwater species.

Fish farmers produce clownfish in great numbers.

The investment of time and energy

One more factor that needs to be addressed before you start setting up your new marine aquarium is the amount of time and energy you'll need to invest to keep it running smoothly. In many ways, an aquarium is like a garden. There are certain regular gardening chores–weeding, pruning, fertilizing, and such–that simply cannot be avoided, no matter how hardy and resilient are your plants. If you leave the garden on autopilot, it will quickly deteriorate into an unsightly mess. The same principle applies to the marine aquarium (or any other aquarium, for that matter). Failing to remove uneaten food, forgetting to replace water lost to evaporation, skipping water changes, or neglecting any other routine maintenance chore can have disastrous consequences on the condition of your tank and the health of the organisms within it, especially when it comes to the mini-reef. This isn't to suggest that you can't squeeze a marine aquarium into an already chaotic schedule. After all, who among us has a light schedule nowadays? However, you may need to create daily and weekly maintenance checklists so you can physically mark off each task once it's been completed. Otherwise, like the garden on autopilot, your beautiful aquarium might start to deteriorate before your very eyes.

Getting the whole family involved

Another way for a busy person to stay on top of aquarium maintenance is to delegate certain routine chores to other family members. Younger kids are generally very enthusiastic about being included in their parents' pastimes, so why not let them take over some of the easier tasks like looking for sick or dead fish, wiping off salt creep, and turning lights on and off? Older kids and teens (if they aren't too ashamed to be related to a fish fanatic) can be tasked with testing specific gravity and water parameters, monitoring water temperature, and rinsing off prefilters. You might even be able to convince your spouse to assist by performing the occasional water change (although personal experience tells me that this is highly unlikely). You'll have to decide whether it's too risky to let anyone else feed your fish. Considering the impact overfeeding can have on your aquarium's water quality and the health of your fish, it might be better to handle this duty yourself.

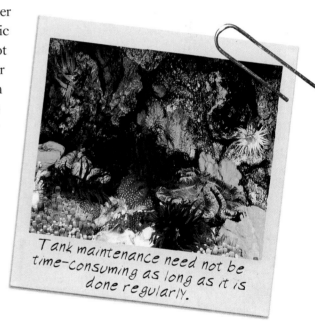

Tank maintenance need not be time-consuming as long as it is done regularly.

Part Two
Getting Started

"Like I always say pal, 'the enemy of my anemone is my friend.'"

Basic Equipment

Okay, we've talked about the benefits of a marine aquarium, the special considerations for beginners and those making the switch from fresh water to salt water, and the amount of time and energy you'll need to invest in order to succeed with your new aquarium. Now it's time to start discussing some of the basic equipment you'll need.

If you haven't done so already, this is an excellent time to decide whether you want to start out with a fish-only tank or to plunge headlong into the mini-reef. The reason for this is that the equipment requirements—especially when it comes to the lighting—are significantly different for each setup. Again, I would be remiss if I didn't attempt to gently

The royal angelfish is not easily fed and rarely survives in the aquarium.

Sailfin tangs are quite hardy as long as they are fed a diet high in algae.

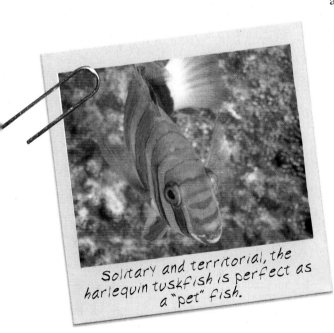

Solitary and territorial, the harlequin tuskfish is perfect as a "pet" fish.

persuade you in the direction of a fish-only tank for your first attempt at a saltwater aquarium. I want you to enjoy success in your new hobby right from the beginning so you'll be encouraged to stick with it for a lifetime, and I'm convinced that this is more likely if you start with fish alone.

A fish-only tank offers a much greater margin of error when it comes to water parameters and will help you to nurture the experience and skills necessary for ultimate success with the reef tank. Besides, you can always convert to a mini-reef after you've gotten your feet wet with fish. On the other hand, if you're a quick study and feel confident of your ability to master reef-keeping techniques on the fly, I wouldn't stand in your way. Just be sure to do some serious research via books, magazines, the Internet, a trusted dealer, and other experienced reef aquarists before experimenting with valuable invertebrates.

Choosing the tank and stand

The most fundamental piece of equipment you'll need for your new marine aquarium is the tank itself. It's critical to choose your tank wisely, since factors like the tank's construction, size, and shape will have an impact on the number and types of organisms you can house within it. Also, the style of tank you choose can either enhance or distort the clarity of the beautiful underwater vista that you're working so hard to cultivate.

All-glass or acrylic?

Tanks used for marine aquarium applications must not contain any materials that will either corrode or release toxic substances when they come into contact with salt water. This immediately rules out those old-fashioned metal-framed tanks, which will quickly rust with

The leaky tank: Use it or lose it?

Just because a glass aquarium leaks doesn't necessarily mean that it's ready for the scrap heap. A more decisive issue is the actual location of the leak. If it occurs along one of the seams between two glass panes or at one of the corners where two side panels and the bottom come together, you may be able to seal the leak with a little silicone aquarium sealant (not to be confused with silicone caulk). However, if one of the glass panes is actually cracked, a repair should not be attempted, especially with larger tanks. In this case, the pressure exerted by the water could cause the pane to shatter, and the result could be a major flood instead of a minor slow leak.

Repairs using silicone aquarium sealant should be performed in a well-ventilated room or, better yet, outdoors where you won't be affected by the powerful fumes. After sealing the leak, give the silicone ample time to cure, according to the manufacturer's recommendations. Follow the manufacturer's directions about the removal of any excess sealant, and rinse the tank repeatedly with fresh water to eliminate any residue.

Even if your leaky tank has to be condemned for aquarium use, you might still find some good uses for it. For example, you could throw in a little potting soil and convert it into a terrarium filled with your favorite houseplants. Or you could cover it with mesh screening and use it as a habitat for a snake, lizard, or turtle.

Part 2

disastrous consequences. It's doubtful that you'd ever come across one of these "antiques" at your local aquarium store, but they still occasionally turn up in garage sales and at flea markets from time to time. If you should happen upon one of these garage-sale specials, or any other used tank of uncertain origin for that matter, do yourself a favor and pass it by–regardless of how irresistible the price may be. You have no way of knowing what was previously kept in the tank or whether it contains some sort of harmful residue that may adversely affect the health of your fish or invertebrates. Of course, it's also difficult to rule out the possibility of leaks without filling the tank with water and observing it for several hours, which is highly impractical in a garage sale or flea market setting.

Given these restrictions, there are two types of tank that are ideally suited for the marine aquarium in terms of construction: all-glass and acrylic, both of which have distinct advantages and disadvantages to consider. Glass tanks are available for sale in a wider

Acrylic is useful for cylindrically shaped aquariums.

Glass vs. acrylic: Which tank should you choose?

Glass	Acrylic
• Available in more stock sizes and designs	• Very shatter-resistant
• Less costly	• Excellent thermal insulation
• Scratch-resistant	• Superior clarity of image
• Heavier (empty)	• More expensive
• Less shatter- and leak-proof	• Scratches very easily

range of stock sizes (anywhere from $2^1/_2$ gallons to over 200 gallons) and designs, and they are relatively inexpensive compared to acrylic—at least until you get into the larger sizes. Glass is also more (but not entirely) scratch resistant. On the downside, glass tanks weigh significantly more when empty, and they are much more likely to shatter or spring leaks. Given their widespread availability and manageable price tag, however, glass tanks make an excellent choice for beginners.

Acrylic tanks offer superior shatter resistance, better thermal insulation, and, because they allow more light to pass through, better clarity with less image distortion. The only real drawback to acrylic tanks, apart from the higher price tag, is the fact that they can be scratched very easily during handling or routine maintenance. Even the seemingly innocuous act of scraping algae off the walls of an acrylic tank can leave annoying scratches. Fortunately, special solvents are available that can be used on acrylic to buff out any scratches.

How big is too big?

The old adage about biting off more than you can chew can be misleading when it comes to the size tank you should buy for your first marine aquarium. In fact, "the bigger, the better" could be a more appropriate rule to live by. Degradation of water quality resulting from decomposing fish waste, overfeeding, overstocking, or the normal metabolic processes of the organisms in the tank is less dramatic in a larger volume of water. This is simply because there is more water to dilute any pollutants or toxic byproducts. Fluctuations in temperature, salinity, and other water parameters are also less pronounced in a bigger tank. Since water quality problems take longer to develop in a big tank, you'll have a greater opportunity to make any necessary adjustments or corrections to counteract them before they reach dangerous proportions.

On the other hand, in a small tank (for our purposes, 29 gallons or less) changes for the worse can occur very quickly, especially when the temptation to stock too many fish wins out over common sense. Unfortunately, this is a very common occurrence among both beginners and experienced aquarists alike. For animals accustomed to life on the coral reef, arguably one of the most stable environments on earth, such rapid changes in water quality are a major source of stress, which can lead to poor health and, ultimately, death.

So how big is big enough? Of course, that depends to a large extent on how much space you have available in your home and how much weight your floors can support, but many experienced marine aquarists recommend starting with at least a 55-gallon tank. Others would argue for a minimum of 75 gallons. Personally, I found 55 gallons to be just about right for my first marine aquarium. In fact, that same tank is still happily humming along with some of its original inhabitants. Does that mean you can't have a beautiful marine aquarium smaller than 55 gallons? Not at all! You'll just have to monitor your water parameters more frequently and perform those routine water changes with even greater diligence.

The shape of success

When shopping for your new tank, assuming you don't have one already, you'll have many different tank designs to choose from, especially if you opt to go with

Tall thin tanks need to be stocked lightly.

Designer tanks are real showstoppers in home or office.

Long, low rectangular tanks can contain more animals than any other shape tank

This is a very sleek, modern design with matching stand and hood.

all-glass. Many aquarium dealers offer hexagonal, octagonal, triangular, and other irregularly shaped tanks as alternatives to the standard rectangular kind. While these tanks are certainly attractive from an interior design standpoint, they aren't necessarily ideal for use as marine aquariums.

For one thing, they tend to be much taller than they are wide. This is a problem for the fish-only aquarium because it restricts the amount of space the fish can use for swimming and establishing territories. Remember, most fish species tend to occupy a particular section of the water column for most of their lives, depending on how their bodies are adapted for feeding. Some are bottom-dwellers, some occupy the mid-water region, and some remain near the surface. Rarely do they move between all three. It stands to reason, then, that a low, rectangular tank with lots of horizontal swimming space would be better for fish.

Sessile invertebrates in the mini-reef aquarium also do better when kept in a low, rectangular tank. This is because the "photosynthetic" corals, anemones, and giant clams that are commonly kept in these setups rely on high-intensity lighting of a particular spectrum in order to survive and thrive. In a tall, narrow tank the light cannot penetrate all the way to the bottom and will benefit only those organisms positioned at the highest point in the tank. To ensure that all of the light-hungry invertebrates get the exposure they need, it's a good idea to keep them in a tank no taller than 20 inches, and a height of 18 inches or less would be even better.

Another drawback to taller, irregularly shaped tanks

is that they have a poor water volume to surface area ratio. In other words, the interface between the aquarium's water surface and the ambient air is much smaller than it is with a rectangular tank of the same volume. This reduces gas exchange between the water and air, which makes it harder to achieve proper oxygenation and to vent noxious gases from the system.

Again, this is not to suggest that you can't have a perfectly satisfactory marine aquarium in a hexagonal or octagonal tank. Just be aware that these tanks have certain design limitations that may affect the number and types of organisms you can safely keep together. Since these tanks are constructed from multiple glass panes positioned at various angles to one another, another consideration is that the aquatic display may be distorted significantly depending on where you're standing in the room–a flaw that may not be readily apparent at the time of purchase.

The stand: buy it or build it?

Once it's up and running, your new aquarium will contain many gallons of water, heavy rockwork and decorations, valued fish and invertebrates, lots of costly equipment, and all of your hopes and dreams of success in the hobby. In other words, it would be safe to say that there's an awful lot riding on the structural integrity of the stand you choose to support your new marine aquarium. Considering the critical (albeit unglamorous) role the aquarium stand plays, you should select it with the same amount of care you use when selecting the tank.

The life-support equipment is well disguised in this coffee-table style aquarium.

As a general rule, it's best to use a commercially manufactured stand designed specifically to support the weight of an operating aquarium. You could choose from the many wooden cabinet-style stands, which tend to blend in well with the interior design of many traditional homes. If you prefer a sleek, contemporary look, you could always go with one of the colored acrylic stands. In some

Custom stands are designed to safely hold the weight of the aquarium.

cases, a suitable stand can be purchased as part of a package deal that includes the tank, the stand, and a matching lighted hood. Sometimes you're almost forced into taking a matching stand with the tank, because the tank might not be guaranteed if you don't buy the stand as well.

As far as building a stand goes, that is something best left to the experienced carpenter or cabinetmaker. Of course, if you have the necessary woodworking skills, there's no reason that you shouldn't try to build your own. I'm just not sure that it's really the most economical approach once you factor in the cost of materials and the time you will have to invest in building it.

Wrought iron and other metal stands are not usually considered appropriate for the marine aquarium. Just like metal-framed aquariums, metal stands will quickly rust when they come into contact with salt water. Even those painted with a protective textured coating are vulnerable to rust in areas where the coating has been accidentally scraped off. I can tell you from experience that once rust gets a foothold on a metal aquarium stand there's no practical way to sand it down and repaint it without getting dust and metal filings in your aquarium's water. (Okay, I'll admit that it sounds silly now, but it sure seemed like a good idea when it first popped into my head!) In addition, metal stands tend to concentrate all of the aquarium's considerable weight onto four small points on the floor, which may cause structural damage, depending on your floor's construction.

Location, location, location
When choosing a site in your home to place your new aquarium, there are several important factors to consider. These include the weight-bearing capacity of the floor, electrical access, the proximity of windows and heat sources, and the amount of traffic that usually passes through the room. You'll also want to take the not-so-remote possibility of water damage into account when picking a location. With any aquarium, occasional spills and drips are almost inevitable, which may rule out rooms with finished hardwood floors, fine rugs, or costly carpeting.

A weighty issue

The first question you'll need to ask yourself about a possible location is whether the floor can support the weight of a functioning aquarium. Each gallon of salt water weighs approximately 8.5 pounds. Add to that the combined weights of the substrate, the rockwork, the filtration equipment, the sump (if one is used), the stand, and the tank, and you've got a substantial amount of weight being exerted over a relatively small area of floor. As a general rule, you can calculate 10 pounds of weight per gallon of tank capacity to arrive at the approximate total weight of an aquarium. Thus, for a 55-gallon aquarium you can safely assume that your floor must be capable of withstanding a minimum constant weight of 550 pounds–and it must do so for (hopefully) many years.

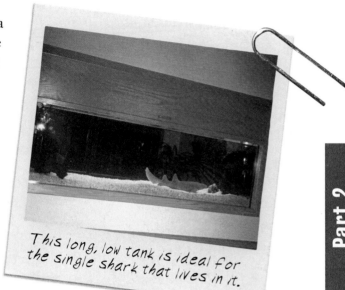

This long, low tank is ideal for the single shark that lives in it.

If your flooring is of concrete or sturdy enough wooden construction, you shouldn't have any problems stemming from the weight of the aquarium. With any wooden floor, however, you should try to distribute the weight of the tank over as many joists as possible for maximum support. If you aren't sure about your floor's load-bearing capacity, especially if you're planning to set up a very large aquarium (or if you're considering putting the aquarium on the second floor), be sure to consult with a building contractor or structural engineer before getting under way.

Keep it on the level

Once your marine aquarium is up and running, it will be for all intents and purposes an immovable object. The last thing you'll want to discover at that point is that the tank is not sitting level on its stand. The only remedy in this situation is to tear the tank down, level it, and start all over again. Otherwise, the tank will be more likely to spring a leak at one of the seams because of the uneven pressure being exerted by the water. It's also a good idea to place a thin sheet of level cushioning material between the aquarium and stand.

Have you got the power?

Even if you intend to set up a basic marine aquarium with very few bells and whistles, you'll still need convenient access to a reliable source of electrical power. At the very least, you'll need to power your lights, heater, and filtration devices, and you'll want to have enough capacity left over so you can expand your equipment arsenal as needed. This last point is especially important if you eventually plan to convert from a fish-only tank to a mini-reef.

I've found that two fully operational 110-volt outlets in close proximity to the aquarium usually are adequate for a basic setup. You can always add a power strip with a built-in surge protector if more outlets are desired. Avoid placing important life-support components on the same circuit with other energy-draining household appliances to avoid overloading the circuit. You don't want to have to make repeated trips to the breaker or fuse box because the circuit keeps blowing. Not only is this inconvenient for you, but it can also upset the delicate balance of your aquarium's water parameters.

It's important to remember that safety is a major issue any time electrical components are used around water. A ground fault circuit interrupter, which will automatically disrupt the flow of current to a device in the event of accidental immersion, should be used in conjunction with all powered aquarium equipment to reduce the risk of electrocution. In addition, it's a good idea to tie a small loop in the middle of your equipment power cords to prevent water and salt buildup (a.k.a. salt creep) from gradually traveling down a cord into an outlet and causing a short. However, this step is unnecessary if the outlets are positioned higher than the aquarium's water surface. In that case, the water and salt would have to fight against gravity to reach the outlet. I find it helpful to wipe off each power cord with a slightly damp cloth each time I perform a routine water change to prevent salt and other gunk from building up in the first place.

This fish is quick on the trigger!

The triggerfish (family Balistidae) is so named because of the locking spine located on its first dorsal fin. When frightened or pursued by a predator, the triggerfish can wedge its laterally compressed body into a crevice in the reef and erect this dorsal spine to lock itself in place. Once this spine is engaged, it becomes nearly impossible for the predator to extract the triggerfish from its refuge. This particular adaptation also makes it extremely difficult to net a triggerfish from an aquarium without first removing much of the rockwork.

Don't let the sun shine in

Try to avoid placing your aquarium in a room with lots of windows that let natural sunlight stream in. If you can manage it, avoid direct sunlight altogether. While you may be tempted to take advantage of natural light to illuminate your new tank for free, especially if your aquarium features "photosynthetic" invertebrates, this is not necessarily the best idea. For one thing, natural sunlight is unreliable and uncontrollable when compared to artificial lighting. It can also fuel unsightly algal blooms and cause your water temperature to fluctuate wildly out of control.

The relative position of heating vents, registers, or space heaters can also influence where you place your aquarium. If the tank is located too close to any of these heat sources, you may have a difficult time regulating water temperature during the winter months. On the other hand, if your home lacks central air conditioning and you live in an area where summer temperatures tend to spike, you might have to place your aquarium in a room that can be outfitted with a window air conditioner or in a spot where the temperature changes aren't so abrupt.

Finally, try to select a cozy, relaxing location where there will not be a constant flow of foot traffic. Excessive activity in the area surrounding the aquarium can be very stressful for the fish within it, and stressed fish are more prone to disease and less likely to exhibit their natural behaviors. It's important that the area be comfortable for you the aquarist because, hopefully, you'll be spending lots of time in front of the aquarium, observing the fascinating interactions of the organisms and admiring the fruits of your labor.

The heat is on!

As I've already mentioned (and likely will again before this book is finished), water parameters on the coral reef are remarkably stable. This applies to not only the chemical composition, salinity, and pH but also the temperature of the water. The ideal temperature range for most marine organisms found on and around the world's coral reefs is between 72 and 79 degrees Fahrenheit. What the aquarist should strive for is to establish a particular temperature within that range that can be fairly consistently

Avoid "gadget overload"

The marine aquarium hobby is rife with high-tech equipment and gadgets, many of which you can live without when you're just getting started—especially if you decide to go with a fish-only aquarium. For example, as you start shopping for equipment you'll probably hear about devices like ozone generators, ultraviolet sterilizers, calcium reactors, and ion exchangers. And that's just a small sampling! While each of these devices can play an important role in your overall water quality and the health of the specimens in your aquarium, they simply aren't necessary for a basic system. Besides, all of these "bells and whistles" can really take a bite out of your aquarium budget. You'll be much happier in the long run if you start out with just the basic equipment and add devices as your confidence grows and your budget allows.

Part 2

Uncouth Crustaceans

To the casual observer, barnacles look and behave more like feather duster worms than crutaceans, having numerous feathery appendages that withdraw with lightning speed into a protective calcareous shell at the first sign of danger. But make no mistake! Barnacles are crustaceans, related to crabs, lobsters, and shrimps. Those "feathery appendages" are actually their feet, which they use to capture drifting particles of food. Eating with their feet? Such manners!

Though barnacles are fascinating to observe in nature (unless you're a boat owner!), they aren't the best choice for the closed system of the aquarium. Their demand for large quantities of miniscule foods can be difficult for the average aquarist to satisfy, and it places a very heavy burden on the filtration system. That being said, some barnacle species have been known to make their way into the aquarium attached to corals or as live rock stowaways.

Barnacles require too much fine food to be well kept in an aquarium.

maintained, factoring in external influences like sun exposure, seasonal changes in air temperature, and the proximity of home heating and cooling appliances.

Avoid the ups and downs

The exact value of the water temperature is not as critical as the stability of the temperature. In fact, it would be better to maintain a consistent temperature of 80 degrees, which is actually outside the ideal range, than to bounce from 74 degrees on one day to 78 degrees the next day and so on. Some seasonal temperature fluctuation is to be expected, however, and most marine organisms will readily adapt to these changes, provided they occur gradually and are not too pronounced.

It's important to note that prolonged temperatures in excess of 84 degrees Fahrenheit can be very stressful to fish and even more so to invertebrates in the mini-reef aquarium, and appropriate steps should be taken to prevent this from occurring. If such a temperature spike is likely due to seasonal influences in your geographic region and you don't have an air conditioner to cool the ambient air, you may need to invest in a chiller unit to help keep the water temperature within the ideal range.

Heating devices

Fortunately for budget-conscious aquarists, heating a marine aquarium is a fairly simple, low-cost proposition. Modern fully submersible heaters combine a thermostat and heating element in a very compact glass tube that can be attached via suction cups (usually included) to one of the glass walls of the aquarium–preferably

What is coral bleaching?

There's no question that the phenomenon known as coral bleaching is occurring with increasing regularity on tropical reefs throughout the world. But even among the experts, there is major disagreement over the actual cause. Most fingers point to prolonged periods of excessively high water temperature as being the root of the coral bleaching problem. Other possible contributing factors include sedimentation, solar irradiation, exposure to air during extremely low tides, and disease.

You'd never guess it by looking at the beautifully colored invertebrates on a coral reef, but the tissues of corals are actually translucent. Their bright colors come from the symbiotic algae—called zooxanthellae—that reside within their tissues and provide the corals with nutrients through the process of photosynthesis. When corals are stressed, due to one or more of the factors listed above, the concentration of zooxanthellae in their tissues may decrease. At the same time, the concentration of photosynthetic pigments within the algae may decrease. The calcareous skeleton of the coral then becomes visible through the translucent tissue—hence the bleached appearance.

However, not all bleaching events are fatal to the corals involved. If the stressor is eliminated or reduced in relatively short order, the zooxanthellae can rebound within a few weeks. Some experts even suggest that bleaching can promote the survival of corals by providing them an opportunity to replace weaker strains of zooxanthellae with more stress-resistant strains.

Part 2

adjacent to the return flow of either the mechanical or wet/dry filter for optimum heat dispersion. Those who prefer to keep all gadgets out of sight for a more natural-looking aquarium can conceal a submersible heater within the rockwork in the main aquarium, with only the cord still visible, or in the sump beneath the aquarium (assuming a wet/dry system is being used).

Some heater models are designed to be clamped to the top edge of the aquarium so that the glass tube extends into the water while the temperature adjustment dial remains above the surface. These heaters operate on the same principle as the submersible kind, but they have one main drawback: because they cannot be fully submerged, they're more difficult to conceal than

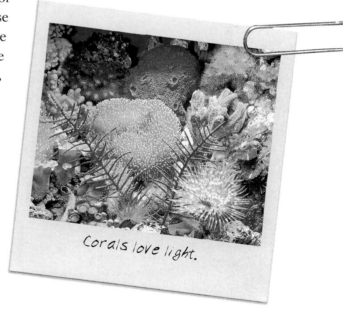

Corals love light.

the submersible style. Also, they tend to be considerably more bulky, which further detracts from the esthetics of the aquarium. Tank-mounted heaters do have advantages, however. The adjustment dial always stays high and dry, so it's easily accessible, and you don't have the problem of algae growing over and obscuring the calibrated temperature settings.

Whichever style of heater you choose, make sure it is constructed of sturdy glass so it can't be easily broken by shifting rockwork or the actions of the organisms in the tank. Also, look for a model that has easy-to-read temperature settings and can be easily adjusted while it is still positioned in the aquarium. You should also give careful thought to ease of access for adjustment and cleaning when deciding where to place the heater.

How do heaters rate?

Aquarium heaters are rated by wattage. The higher the wattage of a given heater, the more rapidly it will raise the temperature of the aquarium water. For example, if it takes 45 minutes for a 200-watt heater to raise the temperature in an aquarium by 5 degrees, it would take $1\frac{1}{2}$ hours to raise the temperature by 5 degrees using a 100-watt heater.

How much heating capacity will you need for your aquarium? As a general rule, you'll want to provide approximately 5 watts of heating capacity per gallon of water for a smaller aquarium and approximately 3 watts per gallon for a larger aquarium. (Remember, temperature is more stable in a larger volume of water.) For a 29-gallon tank, you'd need a heater rated at 150 watts, while a 250-watt heater would be sufficient for a 75-gallon tank. According to some experts, it's better to use two lower-wattage heaters, with each providing half of the necessary heating capacity, than one higher-wattage heater. That way you won't lose all of your heating capacity in the event that one of the units fails.

Stay back, or I'll hurl my guts at you!

Certain sea cucumbers and sea apples of the phylum Echinodermata do something completely unexpected whenever they are threatened, disturbed, or merely unhappy with their living conditions—they eject a toxic gooey substance from their anuses. When released within the confines of the aquarium, this substance can poison or fatally entangle the rest of the organisms in the tank. As an amusing aside, some Pacific Islanders will coat their feet with this rubbery, threadlike substance to protect their soles from sharp rocks and shells while fishing in the shallows.

Beware the hand-me-down heater!

Considering the relatively low price of quality submersible aquarium heaters these days, you're better off purchasing a brand-new unit than using some antiquated model that has been moldering away in your basement or attic for years or one that was handed down from a well-intentioned friend who no longer has a need for it. The trouble with many older heaters is that when they break down they tend to fail in the "on" position. If this happens and you don't catch the problem soon enough, your aquarium's water temperature will rise precipitously, and you may end up losing all of your valued specimens.

Modern heaters, on the other hand, are designed to fail in the "off" position, resulting in a very gradual cool-down to room temperature. Since the average home is heated to somewhere between 70 and 72 degrees Fahrenheit during the winter months, all but the most delicate organisms will most likely survive until you have a chance to replace the faulty heater.

Suction cups keep heaters in place.

Monitoring temperature

Daily monitoring of your aquarium's water temperature, using either a floating or fixed aquarium thermometer, will allow you to detect any trend away from the desired stable setting that you are trying to maintain. Floating thermometers, as the name implies, are designed to be placed directly into the aquarium, where they tend to bob along at the mercy of the water current (assuming some is provided). The only drawback to the floating style is that they often drift into hard-to-reach places, which makes monitoring difficult. I find it convenient to "corral" my floating thermometer within the overflow box of my wet/dry biofilter. That way I always know right where to look for it when I'm in a hurry.

Fixed thermometers come in several styles, many of which attach to the interior glass of the aquarium by means of suction cups. (In fact, many floating models come with suction cups so they can be fixed to the glass as well.) These are handy because they can be positioned so the readout is always facing you instead of the interior of the tank. Also, you can place them at any depth in the aquarium rather than just at the surface–an important detail considering the fact that the temperature at the surface may not coincide with the temperature deeper in the tank, especially if high-intensity lighting is used. In this case, it's

Part 2

Keep an eye on the temperature of the water.

a good idea to use two thermometers, one at the surface of the aquarium and one at the bottom, so you can easily determine whether the heat is circulating properly or not.

Another style of fixed thermometer is the liquid-crystal variety, which is designed to adhere directly to the exterior glass of the aquarium like a sticker. These thermometers are very convenient in the sense that they are easy to read and readily accessible–attributes that have not gone unnoticed by many pragmatic aquarium dealers. One could argue that they aren't quite as accurate when it comes to reflecting the exact temperature as the different models that are designed to be placed inside the aquarium. However, they do reliably indicate whether the temperature remains stable or not, which, as I've mentioned, is more critical than the precise value.

Let There be Light!

Now we're moving into an area–the proper way to light the aquarium–that for many newcomers to the marine aquarium hobby seems to be shrouded in mystery, if not downright perplexing. I should note that the confusion is not limited to beginners. Many a seasoned saltwater aquarist has shaken his or her head in utter bewilderment at the vast array of lighting options available today. All those acronyms–from NO to VHO to PC to MH, and all the combinations thereof, it's no wonder that so many people are left in a state of befuddlement!

As a general rule, the lighting you'll need–not to mention the subsequent impact your lighting system will have on your pocketbook–depends on whether

Many corals depend on zooxanthellae for their colors.

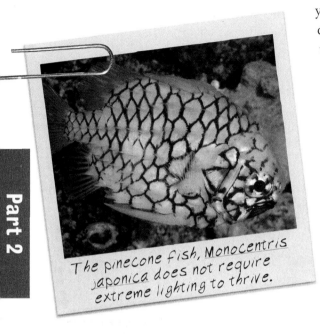

The pinecone fish, *Monocentris japonica* does not require extreme lighting to thrive.

Most blennies appreciate a quiet tank.

you decide to go with a fish-only aquarium or a mini-reef. Each choice will lead you down a very different path when it comes to the intensity level and spectral output of the lamps you'll need to purchase. By diligently researching the specific lighting needs of the marine organisms that you plan to keep (and soliciting the expertise of a trusted dealer) you should be able to make educated, well-considered decisions when you're ready to invest in lamps and fixtures for your aquarium.

Lighting the fish-only aquarium

Fish and non-sessile invertebrates require no special lighting. The only real requirement when illuminating these organisms is to provide sufficient light to display them to their greatest esthetic advantage. In fact, if given overly intense light, some of the more shy and retiring organisms collected from deeper waters will tend to feel exposed and vulnerable, and they may be prompted to disappear from view whenever the lights come on–the exact opposite of the desired result. On the other hand, you wouldn't want to keep the aquarium so dark that the fish assume night has fallen and so remain perpetually hidden in the rockwork in an effort to evade predation.

For the 55-gallon fish-only aquarium we've been using as our basic model up until now, a standard reflective aquarium hood outfitted with a pair of 40-watt normal output (NO) fluorescent lamps is more than adequate. You can even get away with suspending an inexpensive fluorescent utility hood by chains above the tank, provided the top of the aquarium is securely covered with a glass sheet to prevent salt water from splashing onto the lamps.

In previous sections of this book, I've recommended that you avoid using certain obsolete equipment (i.e., metal-framed tanks and antiquated heaters) for your new marine aquarium.

The same suggestion should also apply to those old-fashioned lighted hoods containing incandescent bulbs that long ago fell into disfavor among most aquarists. Incandescent bulbs have two distinct drawbacks when compared to fluorescent tubes. For one thing, most of the energy they produce is in the form of heat rather than light, which means the water temperature will tend to increase when the lights are turned on and decrease when they are turned off. Secondly, incandescent bulbs radiate heavily from the yellow-orange portion of the spectrum. Light of this color may create a warm and cozy atmosphere in your living room or family room, but it won't do much to showcase the natural beauty of your fish.

Lighting the mini-reef

Light plays a much more complex and fascinating role in the mini-reef than it does in the fish-only aquarium. In fact, if denied lighting of the proper spectrum and intensity level, many (but not all) of the organisms commonly kept in these aquariums simply could not survive. This dependence on light strikes many hobbyists as somewhat odd. After all, everybody knows that plants need light in order to produce food through the process of photosynthesis, but what does light have to do with the survival of certain sessile invertebrates, which, as we all agree, are animals? As a matter of fact, along with crystal-clear water conditions, light has almost everything to do with their survival!

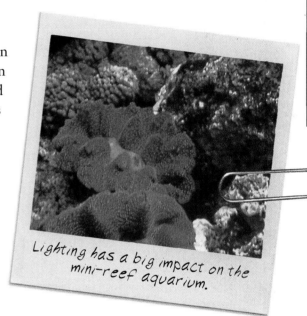

Lighting has a big impact on the mini-reef aquarium.

Share and share alike

Many of the soft corals, hard corals, anemones, and tridacnid clams (the so-called giant clams) that are commonly kept in mini-reef aquariums are considered to be "photosynthetic invertebrates" or "light-hungry invertebrates." Strictly speaking, however, both terms are misleading. It's not the invertebrates themselves that need the light, but rather the symbiotic algae—known as zooxanthellae—that reside within their tissues. The invertebrates rely on the light only indirectly.

Zooxanthellae are actually specialized flagellates (unicellular organisms that move by

Light is critical for the life processes of giant clams.

means of a whip-like extension) that utilize the waste products released by invertebrates (carbon dioxide and ammonia) and energy from the sun to produce simple sugars and carbohydrates through the process of photosynthesis. After utilizing some of these nutrients for their own survival, the algae then share the "leftovers" with their invertebrate hosts. Since the water around a coral reef tends to be very low in dissolved nutrients (as it should be in a mini-reef aquarium as well), both organisms benefit significantly from this relationship. As long as adequate lighting is provided in the aquarium, supplemental feeding of photosynthetic invertebrates is considered by many to be unnecessary, the feeling being that the animals involved get all the nutrients they need from the zooxanthellae residing in their tissues. However, some experienced aquarists feel that the zooxanthellae-equipped inverts need small additional feedings as well.

Artificial sunlight

"Photosynthetic" invertebrates living on tropical coral reefs

They're not all light loving!

Don't let the high cost of mini-reef lighting fixtures discourage you from experimenting with invertebrates. Your dealer can help you choose various sessile invertebrates that have no requirement for special high-intensity lighting but are every bit as interesting as their "light-hungry" cousins. Soft corals of the genus *Dendronephthya* are some of the best choices since they are nocturnal and come from relatively deep waters where light penetration is minimal. There are also numerous anemone species that can thrive in low-light conditions, although they tend to lack the dynamic coloration of the photosynthetic varieties. Beware of anemones belonging to the genus *Aiptasia,* as they can be extremely prolific and may overrun the aquarium. (As a matter of fact, you're probably better off as a beginner by avoiding all anemones, not just the purely pesty *Aiptasia;* even the good-looking anemones cause problems.) And who could forget the fascinating feather duster and Christmas tree worms? Both are indifferent to lighting conditions and will thrive even in a beginner's tank.

There's also a mess of motile invertebrates that have no need for special lighting, including various hermit crabs, cleaner shrimp, sea stars, sea urchins, and algae-eating gastropods. Many of these creatures feel equally at home in either the fish-only aquarium or the mini-reef. Just be careful not to place some of them in the same tank with predatory fish that might view them as hors d'oeuvres!

can rely on natural sunlight to provide lighting of the correct intensity level, spectrum, and duration. Unfortunately, since there's no practical and reliable way to focus natural sunlight on a mini-reef aquarium, it's up to the aquarist to provide an artificial lighting system that replicates the intensity and spectral characteristics of the midday tropical sun as closely as possible.

So how can we go about defining the qualities of tropical sunlight, and how do these qualities relate to the aquarium lighting equipment that is available on the market today?

If you've ever spent too much time sunning yourself on a tropical beach without first applying a liberal dose of sunscreen (at least SPF 30, please!), you've probably already gotten a good sense of just how intense the tropical sun can be–especially if you hail from a more temperate geographic region. But how do we determine the precise level of light intensity–in lumens or whatever unit of measurement lighting specialists use–that is necessary for photosynthetic invertebrates to thrive? The truth of the matter is, we don't have to. To keep things as simple as possible, which is the stated objective of this book, we'll limit our discussion of light intensity to the number of watts produced by a given light source.

You'll want your mini-reef's lighting system to produce a minimum of 3 to 5 watts per gallon of aquarium water. This light level is more than adequate for a basic assortment of soft and hard corals, provided the more light-demanding hard corals are positioned toward the top of the

Christmas tree worms do not require extreme lighting.

The color of the light is very important.

aquarium, where they can derive the greatest benefit. So, following this rule, we'll need between 165 and 275 watts for our 55-gallon tank. Right away, we know that the normal output (NO) lamps recommended for fish-only aquariums would be grossly inadequate for this setup, as four such tubes would provide a total of only 160 watts, and adding more tubes than this is highly impractical. However, there are several high-intensity lighting systems designed specifically for use on reef aquariums, which we will examine in short order.

As previously mentioned, the color spectrum of natural sunlight also plays an important role in maintaining the health of corals and other photosynthetic invertebrates. It stands to reason, then, that you'll want to provide light of similar, or nearly identical, spectral composition for your mini-reef. In order to produce this with artificial lighting, you'll need to choose lamps with a minimum Kelvin (a temperature scale) rating of 5500 degrees (5500K), which is nearly identical to the rating of the midday tropical sun on a cloudless day.

Kelvin temperature is not, as it would appear on its face, a measurement of the heat put out by a given light source, but rather an indication of the spectral output (or wavelength) of the light it produces. At one end of the spectrum you have red (long wavelength), followed by orange, yellow, green, blue, indigo, and violet (short wavelength). Light sources with a higher Kelvin rating emit more of the deeper-penetrating blue-violet portion of the spectrum, which is desirable for most photosynthetic invertebrates, while

Sunlight and salt water

The "white" light emitted by the sun and the artificial light sources we use over our aquariums is not really white at all. Rather, it consists of a spectrum of different colors, each of which corresponds to a particular electromagnetic wavelength and frequency. The longer the wavelength of the color, the shorter the frequency, and vice versa. Colors closer to the red end of the spectrum have longer wavelengths and lower frequencies, while colors closer to the blue end of the spectrum have shorter wavelengths and higher frequencies.

So what does any of this have to do with your marine aquarium? As light penetrates into salt water, the different wavelengths are "filtered out," or absorbed, at different depths. Red, which has the lowest frequency and longest wavelength, is the first to be absorbed, followed by orange, yellow, green, and violet. Blue penetrates the deepest. This information doesn't have much significance for the fish-only aquarium, but if you plan to set up a mini-reef, understanding this characteristic of light will help you to choose lamps with the most appropriate spectral characteristics for photosynthetic invertebrates.

those with lower Kelvin ratings tend more toward the red-yellow portion. Lamps that radiate mostly red and yellow are best avoided, since these colors are the first to be filtered out by sea water and so will not support photosynthetic activity. Also, the red and yellow wavelengths seem to promote the proliferation of undesirable "slime algae."

There are two forms of artificial lighting that reef aquarists commonly utilize to provide the correct intensity level and color spectrum for their light-hungry invertebrates—fluorescent fixtures and metal halide lamps. Both have distinct advantages and disadvantages, depending on the size of the tank they're used on as well as other factors. In general, fluorescent tubes are more convenient, less costly to purchase and operate, and produce considerably less heat while running. On the downside, they don't penetrate water very deeply and thus are used primarily on shallower tanks (20 inches high or less). This drawback can be overcome, somewhat, by increasing the total wattage of the fixture.

Metal halides are the lamps of choice for deeper tanks, since they produce a very intense light that penetrates much deeper in water than can fluorescent lighting, but they, too, have their drawbacks. For one thing, metal halides run exceptionally hot, which necessitates the use of a cooling fan to maintain a stable water temperature. In addition, they can be significantly more expensive to purchase and operate than fluorescents. Which type of lighting is best for your aquarium? Let's take a closer look at both types before we attempt to answer that question.

This is a 10,000 K metal halide bulb.

Power compact lights.

This view is lit with VHO actinic tubes (7100 degrees K).

The same tank after a pair of 5500 K metal halide tubes were added.

Fluorescent options

Fluorescent fixtures generate the most confusion among aquarists looking to light a mini-reef because they are available in such a wide range of sizes, spectra, and power outputs. (Here is where we get into all of those acronyms I mentioned at the beginning of this section!) There's really no reason to let all of the choices overwhelm you, because having more fluorescent options simply means that modern reef enthusiasts have a greater capacity to tailor their lighting systems to meet the specific needs of their photosynthetic invertebrates.

Before we delve into the various fluorescent options for lighting a reef aquarium, it might be helpful to take a brief look at how these lamps actually function. A fluorescent lamp is essentially a glass tube filled with a mixture of inert gases, including argon and tiny quantities of mercury, with an electrode attached to each end (only one end in the case of power compact tubes). The inside of the tube is coated with a powdery phosphor, the exact composition of which determines the ultimate color of the light. When electricity is applied to the tube, an arc of current passes through the gases and vaporizes tiny drops of mercury, causing them to emit ultraviolet light. The UV light then causes the phosphor coating to glow brightly, or fluoresce. The specialized high-intensity fluorescent tubes used for mini-reef aquariums require the use of special electronic ballasts or transformers in order for this process to occur properly.

In terms of power output, fluorescent lamps are rated as being normal output (NO), high output (HO), or very high output (VHO), depending on the number of watts they produce. We've already established that 40-watt NO lamps are not adequate to support the

Part 2

photosynthetic activity of symbiotic zooxanthellae, so we can pretty much rule them out right away. HO tubes, at only 65 watts for a 4-foot tube, are also inadequate for most light-hungry invertebrates. Besides, aquarium dealers seldom offer them for sale anymore. On the other hand, VHO tubes, which provide 110 to 160 watts each (for the 4-foot and 6-foot sizes respectively), are just about right. In fact, two 4-foot VHO tubes placed over our model 55-gallon aquarium will put us well within the desired range of 3 to 5 watts per gallon of water.

Very bright light from a very small package

Another fluorescent option that has gained considerable popularity in recent years is the power compact (PC–a.k.a. compact fluorescent) lamp. As the name suggests, power compacts are much smaller in size than regular fluorescent tubes, which means aquarists can install a larger number of lamps into a single hood for maximum light intensity. They also differ in that only one end of the tube connects to the electrical source.

The three most commonly sold PC lamps have power outputs of 35 watts, 55 watts, and 96 watts respectively. Don't let these relatively low wattages confuse you, however. Due to factors like the size and shape of the tubes and the special electrical ballasts they require for operation, power compacts produce a much brighter light with less wattage than regular fluorescent tubes. For example, a 55-watt PC actually provides more light intensity than a 110-watt VHO. Needless to say, when using power compacts, the 3- to 5-watt-per-gallon rule doesn't apply.

A common combination

One of the more commonly recommended fluorescent lighting combinations consists of VHO daylight (full-spectrum) and actinic blue tubes. Daylight tubes provide the ideal light intensity and color spectrum (similar to that of the tropical midday sun) for light-hungry invertebrates from shallow coral reefs. The actinic blue tubes radiate (surprise!) more of the blue and violet portions of the spectrum that benefit invertebrates from deeper water. If we were to use this particular combination to light our model 55-

Where needed, canopies contain built-in fans to cool the lights.

Modern electronic ballasts are cool and quiet.

Fluorescent lights alone are dim on a marine tank.

gallon mini-reef, one VHO tube of each style would be more than adequate. Many lighting manufacturers also offer fluorescent tubes that are half daylight and half actinic, so you can get "the best of both worlds" from a single tube. Of course, you can also put together a combination of fluorescent tubes and metal halide spots. Your aquarium dealer should be able to help you select the most appropriate combination based on the specific lighting needs of the organisms you intend to keep.

Getting the most from fluorescent lamps

Whichever fluorescent lamps you decide to go with, you can maximize their output by installing them in a hood with a built-in reflector, or you can create a simple light reflector by lining the interior of the hood with smooth aluminum foil. Either approach will capture any light that would ordinarily be lost from the top and sides of the tube and direct it down onto your mini-reef.

You should be aware that all fluorescent tubes tend to lose their lighting efficiency with prolonged use. The longer they burn, the more red their light becomes, and, as we've already established, the red portion of the spectrum is of little value to photosynthetic invertebrates. This shift to red is extremely subtle and cannot be detected with the naked eye. Your invertebrates, however, will notice the difference, and their overall health may begin to decline markedly. Fortunately, all you have to do to avoid this problem is replace your fluorescent tubes on a regular schedule, according to the manufacturer's recommendation. If no replacement schedule is provided, it's a safe assumption that your tubes should be replaced every six months.

More on metal halides

Metal halide lamps are the best lighting choice for mini-reef aquariums over 20 inches tall. Metal halides produce an intensely bright light that is capable of penetrating to the bottom of virtually any size home aquarium. Like VHO daylight fluorescent lamps, metal halides come very close to replicating the color spectrum and light intensity of the midday tropical sun. They typically are mounted in pendant fixtures and suspended above the aquarium, although some are designed for use in full-size fan-cooled hoods in conjunction with fluorescent actinic tubes or power compacts.

With some exceptions, metal halide bulbs look very much like oversized incandescent bulbs. Contained within each bulb are high-intensity discharge tubes that heat up a metal filament when an electrical current is applied. The filament then heats up the gases that are contained in the bulb's core, producing very intense light and lots of heat. The addition of a cooling fan usually is necessary to prevent the water temperature from rising precipitously whenever the lights are turned on. It's also important to keep water from splashing onto metal halide bulbs by placing a tight-fitting glass cover over the top of the aquarium. As with high-intensity fluorescent lamps, metal halides require the use of special electrical ballasts for proper functioning.

In terms of power output, metal halides pack quite a wallop compared to fluorescent lamps. They're most commonly sold in 175-watt, 200-watt, and 400-watt sizes, although lower wattages are available for shorter tanks. Kelvin ratings range from 5500K all the way up to 14000K. As a general rule, you should use one metal halide lamp for every 2 feet of aquarium length. This being the case, two 150- to 175-watt lamps would be just about right for our model 55-gallon aquarium.

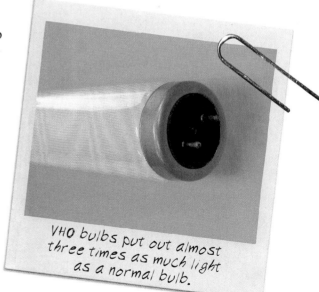

VHO bulbs put out almost three times as much light as a normal bulb.

Metal halide lighting is also very esthetically pleasing. Whereas fluorescent lighting spreads uniformly throughout the aquarium, the light cast by metal halides can be focused on different parts of the mini-reef to create a dramatic interplay of light and shadow.

Not only is this an eye-catching effect, but it also makes it easier to accommodate invertebrates with different lighting requirements in the same tank. For example, animals requiring brighter light, such as hard corals and certain anemones, could be placed directly "in the spotlight" (the anemones will likely migrate there anyway), while certain soft corals and other animals that prefer slightly more subdued lighting could be placed in shadier areas. Metal halides also have the delightful effect of enhancing the rippling movements at the surface of the water, much the way sunlight does on a natural coral reef.

As you delve further into the different lighting options for your mini-reef, you may hear or read accounts of corals and other sessile invertebrates being "burned" by the intense light of

Fluorescent vs. Metal Halide

Fluorescent pros	**Fluorescent cons**
• Less expensive to operate	• Less effective on taller aquariums
• More convenient	• Output may decline unnoticed
• Run cooler	• Require special ballast (except NO)
• Long lasting	
• Available in numerous spectra	
Metal halide pros	**Metal halide cons**
• Ideal intensity level	• Costly to buy and operate
• Suitable for deeper aquariums	• Must be fan cooled
• Enhance rippling effects	• Not necessarily ideal in spectral output
• Create drama of light and shadow	• Require heavy ballast for operation

metal halide lamps. But such claims are somewhat misleading. Even the brightest metal halide lamps can only approximate the intensity of the tropical sunlight that "photosynthetic" invertebrates are accustomed to. True, placing organisms that prefer subdued lighting under metal halides would have a detrimental effect on their health (if you've ever tried to grow shade-loving plants in full sun, you understand exactly what I'm talking about), but such problems stem more from human error rather than any inherent limitations of the lamps themselves.

Sunrise, sunset

Now that we've explored some of the lighting options for marine aquariums, we're faced with another question: what is the optimum photoperiod for both the fish-only aquarium and the mini-reef? In other words, how long should the aquarium lights be left on each day in order for your valued marine organisms to survive and thrive? Here again, the answer depends on the type of system you choose.

For the average fish-only aquarium, six to eight hours of light each day is ample. Remember, apart from establishing a predictable cycle of day and night and giving the fish a little light to feed by, the primary role of the lighting system in a fish-only aquarium is to enhance the aquarist's viewing pleasure. Restricting the photoperiod to between six and eight hours not only helps to keep the growth of undesirable algae in the tank to a minimum but also saves significantly on your energy costs.

Of course, if you want to maximize your enjoyment of the aquarium, it's a good idea to arrange to have the lights turned on–preferably with a little help from an electric timer–when you're most likely to be around. For example, if you usually work from 9 a.m. to 5 p.m., you might want to time your lights so they turn on around 3 p.m. and turn off at 11 p.m. If you work nights, you could schedule them to be on from late morning until early evening. The fish have no preference as to which particular six- to eight-hour period you choose, so it's entirely at your discretion.

There is one scenario where it would definitely be beneficial to leave the lights on for a longer period of time

The PC bulb is made of double fluorescent tubes and is especially bright.

A combination of white and actinic blue is the standard lighting setup.

Part 2

in a fish-only system. That is if you decide to keep tangs or other herbivorous fish in the aquarium. In this case you might want to allow the algae to grow in abundance on the glass (with the exception of the front pane) and rockwork of the aquarium, so the fish can continually graze on the algae throughout the day as they do in nature. You'll just have to be careful not to overfeed these fish so they don't choose to completely ignore the algae growing in the aquarium in favor of the tasty tidbits you offer.

In order for the light-hungry invertebrates in a mini-reef aquarium to really prosper rather than just survive, their symbiotic zooxanthellae need to be photosynthesizing at peak efficiency. Not only do they require lighting of the correct intensity and color spectrum to accomplish this, but also lighting of the correct duration. In fact, even the most costly top-of-the-line combination of fluorescent and metal halide lamps will be of dubious value for a mini-reef if it is turned on for only a short time each day.

A good rule of thumb is to light a mini-reef aquarium for approximately 10 to 12 hours each day. You may need to tweak this lighting schedule somewhat, depending on how the organisms in your aquarium respond over the first few weeks. It's unlikely that "photosynthetic" invertebrates will react adversely to a 12-hour photoperiod, considering the fact that this fairly accurately mimics the lighting cycle of their native tropics. However, if they were deprived of adequate light for a prolonged period, such as during shipping or while with the dealer, or both, they may need some time to adjust to the new lighting routine in your aquarium. If you know or suspect this to be the case, provide only a few hours of light exposure at first and then gradually increase it over several days until the desired level is reached.

Fans are the usual means of keeping the heat from metal halide lights under control.

The proliferation of algae is another factor that may influence lighting duration in a mini-reef system. Algae pose no problem and may be beneficial in a fish-only aquarium, but if allowed to grow unchecked in a mini-reef, these minuscule plants can really wreak havoc, growing over every surface in the aquarium, including the invertebrates themselves. When this occurs, the algae can out-compete the corals and other invertebrates, to the great detriment of the beneficial symbiotic algae residing in their tissues.

Keeping it Clean

On a tropical coral reef, the waste products of the fish and invertebrates are so efficiently utilized by the various indigenous organisms that they have almost no perceptible effect on the quality of the water surrounding the reef. In fact, a marine biologist once told me, "Every piece of fish poop goes through a minimum of three guts on the coral reef before its nutritional value is finally used up." This may be a bit of hyperbole, but there's no question that an incredible diversity of organisms inhabits the coral reef, forming a very complicated food "web," and even the most insignificant scrap can play a major role in the survival of numerous tiny creatures. In addition, any waste matter that somehow manages to escape the attention

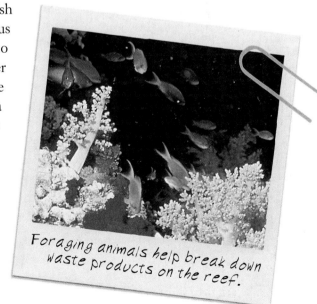

Foraging animals help break down waste products on the reef.

Conscientious attention to water quality results in a dynamite aquarium.

of scavengers is quickly diluted by the vast quantity of water that the ocean comprises.

In the artificial closed system of the marine aquarium, on the other hand, you cannot rely solely on foraging animals for the breakdown of solid waste products (although this may occur to a very small degree in a mini-reef containing live rock and live sand), and there is no instant dilution of liquid waste, dissolved organic compounds, and the harmful byproducts of the nitrification process (much more on nitrification later) as there is in the open ocean. This means that without diligent intervention on the part of the aquarist, organic waste will decompose within the aquarium system, leading to the rapid deterioration of water quality.

What's so important about water quality?

In the fish-only aquarium, poor water quality usually leads to stressed fish, and stressed fish are much more susceptible to bacterial, viral, and fungal illnesses and parasitic infestation. Of course, when the fish get sick, the aquarist usually goes into a panic and responds by dosing the aquarium with various and sundry medications, some of which are actually more harmful to the fish than the disease itself–a sort of vicious cycle that, more often than not, results in the heartbreaking loss of valued specimens.

An ounce of prevention

When it comes to the health of your valued marine specimens, it's always better to be proactive than reactive. Taking the necessary steps to satisfy the three major forms of filtration—mechanical, chemical, and biological—and staying on top of those routine partial water changes will not only keep your marine aquarium's water looking crystal clear but also will help to keep your fish or invertebrates in excellent health. On the other hand, inadequate filtration and inconsistent water changes inevitably lead to the outbreak of disease, which usually sends the aquarist scrambling to the nearest aquarium store to buy an assortment of costly medications. If the disease is misidentified, as often happens, the wrong medication might be administered, and the cure may end up being worse than the disease.

Part 2

In the mini-reef aquarium, very exacting, almost pristine water conditions must be maintained at all times. As I've mentioned repeatedly, stability is the rule on the coral reef, and this applies equally to the water quality in the mini-reef. Even a slight degradation in water conditions, which would probably have little or no significant impact in a fish-only system, could spell disaster for an aquarium full of invertebrates–just another subtle hint that you might be better off getting your feet wet with a fish-only aquarium first!

So what steps can you take in order to maintain excellent water quality in your new marine aquarium? First, you'll need to familiarize yourself with the three basic forms of filtration–mechanical, chemical, and biological–and the different types of equipment you can use to achieve them. You'll also want to develop a basic understanding of the process of protein skimming, which is possibly one of the most significant technical advances the marine aquarium hobby has seen in recent years. Finally, it is very important to understand that no amount of filtration gadgets can take the place of routine partial water changes. Whether you decide to go with a fish-only aquarium or a mini-reef, the one sure way to remove pollutants before they begin to degrade water quality is to physically siphon out a portion of the dirty water and replace it with clean water. That being said, let's move ahead and begin our analysis of the three forms of filtration.

Mechanical filtration

Mechanical filtration is the easiest of the three forms to understand, primarily because you can actually observe the process and its results with the naked eye. The job of the mechanical filter is a simple one– to physically strain out and remove particulate waste

Protein skimming is the most important advance in modern marine aquariology.

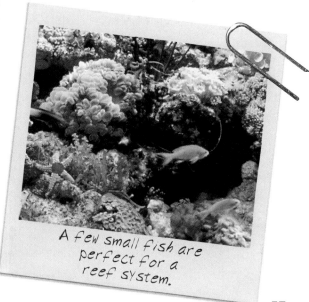

A few small fish are perfect for a reef system.

Part 2

(fish feces, uneaten food, etc.) from the aquarium system. The step of eliminating particulate matter is important for two reasons. For one thing, debris clouding the water and accumulating on the rockwork and substrate detracts significantly from the esthetic beauty of the aquarium and therefore reduces the pleasure the aquarist derives from it. More importantly, any dirt and debris left in the system will decompose and foul the water in short order. The two mechanical filtration devices most frequently used for marine aquarium purposes nowadays are the hang-on-tank filter and the canister filter, each of which has its pros and cons.

Pros and cons of the hang-on-tank filter

The hang-on-tank filter is essentially a plastic box that hangs on the outside of the aquarium on the side or the back of the tank, depending on the configuration of the other equipment in the system. The box is divided into two chambers, one larger and one smaller. The larger chamber contains the various filter media (foam sponges, fiber pads, spun nylon floss, etc.), while the smaller chamber contains a siphon tube. One end of the tube is attached to an impeller, which is powered by a small electric motor located on the underside of the smaller chamber, and the other end of the tube extends down into the aquarium water.

When power is applied to the motor, the impeller begins to rotate rapidly, forcing the air out of the tube and drawing water up from the aquarium into the small chamber. From there, the water spills over into the larger chamber, where it is filtered through the various media and then returns to the tank under the influence of gravity. You may encounter hang-on-tank models that deviate from this theme, but the same basic principle–take the water out of the tank and into the filter, strain it, and then return it to the tank–usually applies.

Mechanical filtration "in a clamshell"

Mechanical filtration is the process of physically straining suspended particulate matter out of your aquarium's water—usually by passing the water through a sponge, filter floss, or a similar medium contained within a power filter, whether of hang-on-tank or canister type. It's necessary for two very important reasons:

- It prevents unsightly debris from clouding the water and accumulating on the rockwork, decorations, and substrate.

- Suspended particulate waste is removed promptly from the system, so it cannot decompose and degrade the aquarium's water quality.

Can you get by without mechanical filtration? To a certain extent you can— if you're extremely diligent about partial water changes. But you'll be much happier with your water quality and the look of your aquarium if you include some form of mechanical filter in your water purification system.

The biggest advantage of the hang-on-tank filter is its ease of use. Literally within minutes of removing the filter from its package, you can have it up and running on your aquarium. All you have to do is hang the box in the desired location, snap a few lengths of plastic tubing together, attach the siphon to the impeller mechanism, add the desired filter media, fill the filter box with aquarium water, plug in the power cord, and you have mechanical filtration! Because hang-on filters are so easy to use, many beginners prefer them. They're also popular, because of their familiarity, with many experienced aquarists making the switch from freshwater to saltwater.

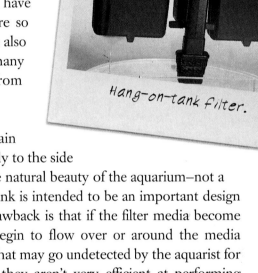

Hang-on-tank filter.

However, hang-on-tank filters do have certain limitations. For example, since they mount directly to the side or back of the tank, they tend to detract from the natural beauty of the aquarium—not a major drawback, but an issue of concern if the tank is intended to be an important design element or showpiece in the home. Another drawback is that if the filter media become clogged with dirt and debris, the water may begin to flow over or around the media without being filtered effectively, an occurrence that may go undetected by the aquarist for a long time. Also, they lack versatility in that they aren't very efficient at performing chemical and biological filtration. In other words, hang-on-tank filters are best viewed as dedicated mechanical filters only.

Pros and cons of the canister filter

If you want more versatility from your mechanical filter, an external (outside-the-tank) canister filter may be your best option. A canister filter is—as the name implies—a closed plastic canister designed to hold various filter media. Often several removable compartments are included with the canister to make the separation of media easier and more practical. Within most canisters is a pump housing containing a motor and impeller, although the pump is separate with some models. Water is gravity fed from the aquarium through a siphon hose down into the canister, which is usually situated below the water level of the aquarium. There it is pumped under pressure through the various filter media and back into the aquarium through a return hose.

Part 2

Canister filters can be hidden out of sight.

Canister filters can be plumbed together in a series.

The advantages of canister filters over hang-on-tank models are numerous. For one thing, they are much less disruptive in terms of esthetics. In fact, they can be placed completely out of sight inside a cabinet-style aquarium stand (or any desired location in reasonable proximity to the aquarium, for that matter) with only the supply and return hoses showing. They're also much more versatile: by placing mechanical, chemical, and biological filtration media into separate compartments within a single canister, you can achieve all three forms of filtration with one space-saving unit. Also, some canister filters are designed so that multiple units can be plumbed together in a series and powered by a large external pump. So, for example, you could place mechanical filtration media in the first canister, biological filtration media in the second, chemical filtration media in the third, and so on. Such a setup is ideal for filtering very large tanks or several smaller tanks simultaneously.

Of course, canister filters also have their drawbacks. Whereas hang-on-tank filters are extremely easy to install and operate, canister filters can seem a little more complicated and off-putting to the beginning aquarist. This anxiety isn't completely unjustified. Water under pressure tends to follow the path of least resistance, so if a canister filter is not properly assembled and one of its O-rings fails, the result could be major flooding. Also, canister filters pose more of a challenge when it comes to routine maintenance. You can't simply shut off the system and pop off the hoses without spraying water all over everything, so it is necessary to install a series of cutoff valves that allow you to isolate both the canister and plumbing when it's time to clean the canister or replace the filter media. Newer canister filter models are dealing with this disadvantage.

Pros and cons of the undergravel filter

Aquarists who are crossing over from fresh water to salt water are likely to be familiar with the undergravel (UG) filter. The UG filter, often referred to in aquarium literature as the "old workhorse" of aquarium filtration, was the filter of choice for many years among both freshwater and marine aquarists. However, it has recently fallen out of favor, largely due to newer filtration technologies that have since swept the aquarium industry.

At this point, you might be asking yourself why, if undergravel filters were considered to be reliable and effective in the past, the same shouldn't be true now. Indeed, many experienced freshwater aquarists, and quite a few "old salts" returning to the hobby after being out of it for many years, might ask the same question. Actually, it's not that UG filters are any less reliable or effective, but rather that some of the newer filtration systems just tend to get the job done better, especially when it comes to mechanical filtration.

The basic UG filter system consists of a plastic perforated plate with transparent plastic lift tubes attached along the back edge at each corner. This unit is placed on the bottom of the tank and covered with a suitable crushed coral or aragonite substrate. A recirculating water current is created by either airstones, which are placed inside the lift tubes and connected to an air pump, or powerheads mounted on top of the lift tubes. Both methods cause the water to flow up the lift tubes, discharge from the tubes at the water surface, and travel down through the substrate into the filter plate. The only difference between the two methods is that powerheads pump the water much more forcefully, creating a fairly substantial current.

With a UG system, suspended particulate matter is drawn down into the substrate, where it is mechanically filtered out of the water. Biological filtration takes place at both the substrate level and in the perforated plate below the gravel. Ironically, the mechanical filtration aspect of a UG filter can actually work against its effectiveness as a biological

This is an undergravel filter with crushed coral.

filter. As more and more debris is drawn down into the substrate, the perforations in the filter plate can become clogged, thereby creating "dead spots" and discouraging the colonization of the beneficial aerobic bacteria necessary for biological filtration. Decomposing solid waste trapped within the substrate and filter plate can also have a serious impact on water quality–a fact that has not been lost on many reef aquarists, who typically shun UG filters in favor of other systems. For these reasons, it is very important when using a UG filter to vacuum the substrate frequently with a siphon hose.

If you're not discouraged by their limitations and still want to go with an undergravel filter, your best bet is to set it up as a reverse-flow system to prevent the filter plate from clogging in the first place. The most effective way to achieve this is by using the return hose of a canister filter to pump the water down through the lift tubes and up through the filter plate and substrate. This keeps particulate waste suspended in the water where it can be effectively eliminated by the canister filter. And since solid waste cannot accumulate to create "dead spots," the biological filter has a chance to become fully established with no interference.

Chemical filtration

Contrary to what the name might suggest, chemical filtration does not involve adding chemicals to the water to eliminate or neutralize pollutants. Rather, when most aquarists discuss chemical filtration, they are referring to the use of a substance known as activated carbon to remove dissolved organic compounds from the aquarium water. You won't need to purchase any additional high-tech gizmos or gadgets to achieve this, since most standard filtration devices, including canister filters, hang-on-tank filters, and wet/dry systems, can accommodate activated carbon along with the various media needed for mechanical and biological filtration.

So what is activated carbon, and how does it filter your water? Essentially, activated carbon is a substance created by baking certain materials, such as wood, coal, and bone at extremely high temperatures. As these

Chemical filtration in a clamshell

When aquarists speak of chemical filtration, they're usually referring to the use of activated carbon to remove dissolved organic compounds. As aquarium water flows through the highly porous activated carbon, which can be placed in most filtration devices, molecules of various undesirable compounds are adsorbed (not absorbed as with a sponge) from the water. In other words, they bond chemically with the carbon. The dissolved compounds can then be effectively eliminated from the aquarium system by simply replacing the carbon once it's been completely used up.

materials bake, tiny pores are opened up, greatly increasing the surface area of the substance. At the same time, the surface of the carbon is chemically altered so that it has the tendency to attract the molecules of various dissolved substances.

When activated carbon is placed in your aquarium's filtration system–preferably sandwiched between two layers of filter floss or inside a nylon stocking to prevent the tiny pieces from being discharged into the aquarium–the water flows through the numerous tiny pores within the carbon, and the dissolved compounds are adsorbed (not to be confused with "absorbed") from the water. That is, the compounds actually form a chemical bond with the surface of the carbon and are effectively eliminated from the system.

Activated carbon in a pre-filled pouch---clean and easy to use.

Heated debate sometimes rages over the value of activated carbon in the aquarium. Such disputes usually stem from the fact that activated carbon will attract and remove both desirable and undesirable compounds equally. In other words, it has no way to discriminate between those substances that are toxic to fish and invertebrates and those that would benefit them, including certain medications, trace elements, chemical buffers, and vitamin supplements.

In addition, the incredible amount of surface area that activated carbon provides is highly "attractive" to the beneficial bacteria that perform biological filtration, which means that each time the carbon is removed, a certain portion of the biological filter goes with it. This is not a significant problem, however, as long as you replace the carbon fairly frequently and provide enough biological filtration elsewhere in the aquarium system to compensate for the loss.

Rinse carbon before you use it in the aquarium.

Beyond activated carbon

Activated carbon is not the only product on the market that can be used to chemically filter your aquarium water. There are also various resin-treated pads and granular filter media that are designed to eliminate specific undesirable compounds, such as ammonia, nitrate, phosphate, or silicate. These products can be effective as long as they are promptly replaced whenever they become exhausted and each one is used in conjunction with its associated test kit. However, it's important to remember that no form of mechanical filtration can take the place of routine aquarium maintenance and, of course, regular partial water changes.

So how much activated carbon is needed to carry out the process of chemical filtration efficiently? Actually, there is no specific way to calculate an exact quantity that is appropriate for a given volume of water. This is due in large part to the fact that not all activated carbons are created equal. As a general rule, you should try to avoid carbons that look shiny and are relatively smooth to the touch. These carbons lack the large amount of surface area found in the rough, dull-looking carbons. Sure, you can save a little money by using an inferior grade of carbon, but you probably won't be happy with the results in your aquarium. Also, the biological load (the number and size of the fish and/or invertebrates in the aquarium) will have a significant impact on how hard the activated carbon actually has to work to chemically filter the water.

Although there's no hard and fast rule governing the amount of activated carbon to use, it is important to replace the carbon regularly according to the manufacturer's recommended schedule. This will prevent the adsorbed toxins from being released back into the aquarium system to the detriment of the fish or invertebrates. It will also limit any impact on the aquarium's biological filtration capacity.

Biological Filtration:
Your Fish Just Can't Live Without It!

Technically, the concept of biological filtration belongs in the "Keeping it Clean" chapter along with mechanical and chemical filtration. However, since your ultimate success in the marine aquarium hobby depends to a great extent on how well you understand and apply this form of filtration, I feel that it deserves a separate chapter of its own.

Biological filtration–also called nitrification–is arguably the most important yet least understood of all the processes we will discuss in this book. For many aspiring aquarists, it's also one of the most mysterious–mostly because the actual nitrification process is invisible to the naked eye, but also because it's carried out by microorganisms, which

A powder blue tang is a big fish that needs big filtration.

Part 2

we typically associate with filthiness and ill health. But, as you'll soon see, there's nothing mysterious about biological filtration, and you certainly don't need to be a microbiologist to understand it.

It's all about bacteria

Nitrification is carried out by beneficial aerobic (needing oxygen) bacteria, known as nitrobacters. The process begins with the release of ammonia into the aquarium water in the form of either excreted fish waste or decomposing organic material (usually uneaten food). It also appears as a result of the natural metabolic processes of aquatic organisms. Ammonia in its pure form is extremely toxic to both fish and invertebrates and will soon cause their death if not quickly converted into less harmful byproducts. The bacteria that utilize ammonia as a food source quickly "go to work" and convert it into a compound called nitrite. Nitrite, though slightly less toxic than ammonia, is still very harmful to fish and invertebrates, so it too must be eliminated from the aquarium water. That's where the next group of bacteria comes in. As soon as the ammonia is converted to nitrite, hungry colonies of bacteria break it down into nitrate–the final byproduct of nitrification.

Most marine fish can tolerate a moderate level of nitrate, provided it accumulates gradually over time, but nitrate is highly toxic to many sessile invertebrates even at low levels. Nitrate also functions as a source of nutrition for plants and can promote blooms of undesirable algae–again, not necessarily a problem for the fish-only tank, but a potential disaster in the mini-reef.

Biological filtration in a clamshell

Biological filtration—arguably the most important form of filtration—is essentially the breakdown of ammonia into less toxic byproducts by beneficial aerobic bacteria. The process goes as follows:

- Ammonia is released into the water through fish waste, decomposing food, a dead fish or invertebrate, etc.

- Nitrobacters convert the ammonia to nitrite, which is slightly less toxic than ammonia but still deadly.

- Other nitrobacters convert nitrite to nitrate, which is toxic to sessile invertebrates but tolerated in moderate concentrations by fish.

- Nitrate is removed from the system through a partial water change, denitrifying filter media, or some form of natural nitrate reduction.

But if nitrate is the final result of nitrification, how do you go about eliminating it before it reaches a hazardous level? You can purchase special nitrate-removing granular filter media or resin pads to chemically filter it from the water, but you'll get mixed results at best with this approach. There is also a natural method you can use to reduce nitrate, which we'll explore in a later section. But for all practical purposes, the only truly reliable way to eliminate nitrate from the aquarium system is to perform a partial water change. And since the water change is the simplest and most reliable solution to the buildup of nitrate, it's the one I would strongly encourage for the beginning marine aquarist. After all, this is supposed to be a Simple Guide, right?

Where do nitrifying bacteria come from?

Okay, we now know that we need special nitrifying bacteria to perform the vital job of biological filtration for us. So how does one go about getting them into the aquarium? The beauty of it is, you don't have to do anything to get them there. They're already in there–on the glass, in the substrate, on the rockwork, and on any other available surface–albeit in relatively small quantities. All you have to do is give them adequate time to flourish and provide the three basic requirements for their survival: food, oxygen, and surface area.

Providing the food source for nitrifying bacteria is a relatively simple proposition, since they "feed" on the byproducts of fish waste and decomposing organic matter. The only time this becomes tricky is when you're first setting up the aquarium, and you haven't introduced any organisms yet. But don't worry. We'll cover that in much greater detail in the section about "cycling" the aquarium.

Since nitrifying bacteria are aerobic, they must be given oxygenated conditions in order to thrive. Usually this is accomplished by creating turbulence at the water surface, such as that produced by the water discharging back into the tank from the various filtration devices. If this is not adequate, oxygenation can be achieved through surface agitation by pumping air through an airstone placed at the bottom of the aquarium. A bubbling airstone can also add to the overall esthetic beauty of the aquarium if the stone is cleverly concealed within the rockwork or decorations and only the bubbles are visible.

Life support for nitrifying bacteria

In order for the beneficial nitrifying bacteria that are responsible for biological filtration to thrive, three essential elements must be provided in the aquarium system—a source of fuel, oxygenated conditions, and abundant surface area on which the bacteria congregate.

- The fuel they need is nitrogenous waste, which is always present in a stocked aquarium in the form of fish waste and decomposing food.

- Oxygenated conditions are provided by the various filtration devices, which create turbulence at the surface of the aquarium as they pump filtered water back into the tank, or by a bubbling airstone.

- Surface area is provided by the substrate, rockwork, decorations, glass, and various biological filtration media.

Part 2

The Nitrogen Cycle

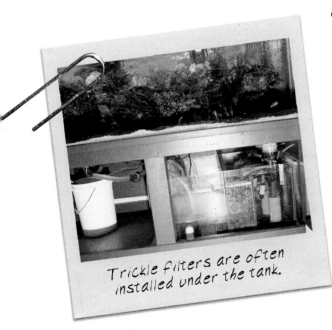

Trickle filters are often installed under the tank.

Surface area is also easy to provide. As I've mentioned, nitrifying bacteria will colonize virtually every surface in the aquarium as long as oxygenated conditions and nitrogenous wastes are made available. You can give the bacteria even more surface area to colonize by inserting some sort of biological filtration medium into your mechanical filter or by including a wet-dry filter in your overall filtration arsenal.

But this brings up another important question: if nitrifying bacteria will colonize the aquarium anyway, why buy a special wet-dry filter to do the job? As with any other issue in the marine aquarium hobby, there are (at least) two schools of thought on the subject. Some insist that wet-dry filters are redundant and therefore unnecessary, while others believe that if a little biological filtration is good, more must be better. I personally fall into the "more is better" category when it comes to biological filtration. Besides, I'm more convinced by the outstanding water quality I've enjoyed since adding a wet-dry filter to my fish-only aquarium than by any arguments against these systems.

What is a wet-dry filter?

Wet-dry filters, also called trickle-down filters, might more accurately be called wet-moist filters, since there's no stage in the system where conditions are totally dry. The "dry" part of the name actually comes from the fact that the filter media are never completely submerged in water. Rather, the aquarium water is allowed to trickle gradually over the various filter media, keeping them constantly moist and highly oxygenated—perfect conditions to encourage the proliferation of nitrifying bacteria.

How do these systems work? Though there are many different styles of wet/dry filter available, each operates on the same basic principle. Since there's no reasonable way to describe the subtle distinctions between each type of filter without lulling you into a coma, I'll limit my analysis to one of the more common designs.

With this type of system, there is a two-chambered box hung on the side of the aquarium. One chamber hangs inside the tank, just slightly below the surface of the water, and the other hangs outside the tank. Water enters the first chamber through a series of slots along its front edge and is drawn into the outside chamber through a constant-level siphon. There the water may pass through a sponge pre-filter to remove any particulate matter before passing, under the influence of gravity, into a flexible tube connected to the bottom of the exterior chamber. The tube transports the water down into the bio-filter, which usually sits beneath the main tank in a separate reservoir, or sump (typically a 10-gallon aquarium).

Assorted filter media.

Once the water reaches the biofilter (a transparent glass or acrylic box divided into two chambers, one upper and one lower) it spreads onto a perforated filter plate located in the top chamber of the box and trickles down over the various bacteria-rich filter media, which are contained in the lower chamber. Additional mechanical and/or chemical filtration media can also be placed in the top chamber to keep the biofilter medium as free from impurities as possible. After being filtered by the nitrifying bacteria, the water collects in the sump and is pumped back into the aquarium through a return hose.

Media for the bio-filter

To encourage the establishment of aerobic nitrifying bacteria, the substance you choose as your biofilter medium must provide ample surface area. This means that the more porous the substance is, the better it will support bacterial colonization. Suitable media include, among other things, sponges, porous ceramic sandglass, spun nylon floss, and heavily grooved plastic spheres that provide an incredible amount of surface area for their size and, hence, ample opportunity for nitrifying bacteria to set up camp.

Part 2

How do the different filters rate?

	Mechanical	Chemical	Biological
Hang-on-tank	Excellent	Poor	Poor
Canister	Excellent	Good	Good
Undergravel	Poor	Poor	Excellent
Wet/dry	Poor	Excellent	Excellent

Natural Nitrate Reduction: have we found the "holy grail?"

I mentioned earlier that there is a method, apart from frequent costly water changes (though regular water changes are encouraged regardless), that you can use to eliminate nitrate from your aquarium without the need for any chemical resins or granular denitrifying filter media. This method, called Natural Nitrate Reduction (NNR), requires the installation of a so-called plenum system beneath the substrate of your aquarium during the initial setup phase.

Filter floss is often used for mechanical filtration.

NNR, a process conceived in the 1980's by Dr. Jean Jaubert of the University of Nice, made a pretty big splash a few years back, with much of the popular aquarium literature heralding it as one of the most significant advances the hobby had seen since the development of synthetic sea salt mixes. Jaubert's method gained even wider popular acceptance with the endorsement of aquarium industry "heavy hitters." However, as with so many advances in the marine aquarium hobby, it wasn't long before articles questioning the value of NNR and plenum systems began to pop up.

So which viewpoint is more accurate? I would suggest that both are correct to a certain degree. In fact, I would argue that every form of aquarium technology has both its selling points and its drawbacks, and all we aquarists can do is to try to make the most educated decisions possible when it comes to the technology that is available to us.

What is a plenum?

The Jaubert method utilizes a stagnant area, known as a plenum, beneath a sand substrate. The plenum is created using a grid material like eggcrate or a standard undergravel filter plate. The grid should be elevated a minimum of one inch off the bottom of the tank (the larger the tank, the deeper the plenum), and there should be a 1-inch gap between the grid and aquarium glass on all sides so the plenum is not visible from outside the aquarium. To achieve the desired height and provide sufficient support for the overlying sand and rockwork, you'll need to affix sections of half-inch-diameter PVC tubing to the bottom of the plenum, using aquarium-safe silicone adhesive or plastic cable ties. Next, wrap the plenum with a sheet of fiberglass window screening to keep the sand from sifting down into the stagnant area, which would reduce its efficiency.

After the plenum is assembled and put in place, it's time to put in the first layer of substrate. This layer should be approximately 2 inches deep and ideally should consist of aragonite or crushed coral sand. Finally, place a second sheet of screening on top of the first sand layer, and top it off with 2 additional inches of sand. The dividing screen between the two layers of substrate is not absolutely essential, though it does help to prevent digging or burrowing organisms from disturbing the lower substrate where the actual nitrate reduction occurs.

That trickster, the false cleaner.

A Case of Mistaken Identity

It's not unusual for larger predatory fish to line up at coral reef "cleaning stations," waiting their turn to be picked clean of parasites by cleaner wrasses (*Labroides dimidiatus*) and other cleaner organisms. The trusting host fish may even allow the diminutive cleaner wrasses to explore inside its oral cavity and gill covers in search of edible tidbits.

But in some cases, what looks like a cleaner wrasse actually turns out to be a false cleaner (*Aspidontus taeniatus*)—a predatory blenny that cleverly mimics the shape and color of the cleaner wrasse. The false cleaner uses this disguise to win the trust of its unsuspecting host and rewards it by promptly biting off a chunk of flesh—a painful case of mistaken identity!

Part 2

Once your aquarium is up and running, you'll need to practice a little patience while the sand becomes colonized with denitrifying bacteria. You can accelerate the process by adding a few handfuls of sand from an established plenum system or by using live sand, which is essentially sand harvested from the ocean floor that contains an array of tiny benthic (bottom-dwelling) marine organisms, including the desired nitrate-reducing microbes.

How does NNR work?

In very simple terms, the plenum serves as a reservoir for a small amount of oxygen and nitrate. There is just enough oxygen to maintain the necessary anoxic (low in oxygen, but not completely anaerobic) conditions in the overlying sand layer to promote the growth of denitrifying bacteria. The nitrate diffuses into the sand layer above the plenum, where the bacteria convert it into free nitrogen gas, which is then released harmlessly from the water at the surface of the aquarium. Other beneficial processes can be attributed to the plenum method as well, including the supplementation of calcium and certain trace elements without the need for commercial additives. Of course, I must emphasize that this is a very rudimentary explanation of the nitrate reduction process, and there is much about the way these systems function that is yet to be fully understood–even among experts.

This filter uses a micron bag to trap fine particles.

Is NNR the best approach for beginners?

So the question is: should you attempt to use Jaubert's method of nitrate reduction in your first marine aquarium? The answer depends on a couple of factors. The first is the type of aquarium you intend to set up–fish-only or mini-reef. Since we've established that most tropical marine fish can tolerate moderate nitrate levels, one could argue that a plenum would be unnecessary in a fish-only system, although there is ample evidence to suggest that plenums can be very effective in fish-only systems, provided stocking levels aren't too excessive. The invertebrates in a mini-reef, on the other hand, are very sensitive to nitrate and may benefit significantly from a system that reduces nitrate before it can accumulate to even moderate levels.

Another question you have to ask yourself concerns whether you are confident enough in your tinkering ability. In other words, are you certain that you'll be able to design and assemble the plenum system correctly? Using improper materials for the plenum or simply putting the materials together the wrong way can result in disaster. For example, if you decided to use a different screening material that tends to clog easily instead of the recommended fiberglass window screening, you could end up creating an anaerobic (rather than anoxic) state in the lower sand layer. This could potentially lead to the buildup of hydrogen sulfide gas and the poisoning of the animals in the aquarium.

So in answer to the initial question about whether or not it is appropriate for the novice marine aquarist to use a plenum system, I would have to say, "perhaps," and I would strongly encourage anyone wishing to experiment with such a system to do so under the watchful eye of a trusted dealer. But if you have any doubts, stick with water changes!

Part 2

More is Best: Skimming and Living Filters

Next to the biofilter, the single most important piece of equipment for the marine aquarium is the protein skimmer, or foam fractionator. In fact, one could conceivably maintain a tank full of marine organisms in superior health using only these two forms of water purification in conjunction with frequent partial water changes.

The purpose of the protein skimmer is to remove dissolved organic waste from the water before nitrifying bacteria act upon it, thereby taking some of the load off the biofilter and slowing the accumulation of nitrate. Protein skimmers are especially efficient at removing surface-active compounds (surfactants), which can usually be seen

This is an airstone driven protein skimmer.

Protein skimming, nature's way

Virtually every process that is carried out in the closed system of the marine aquarium has a parallel component in nature. For example, while aquarists use mechanical protein-skimming devices to remove dissolved organic compounds from aquarium water, Mother Nature combines the forces of wind and waves to remove these pollutants from natural bodies of water. If you've ever noticed dirty foam collecting on a beach during a windstorm or at the base of a weir or waterfall, you've seen this natural protein skimmer at work.

This is natural skimming on the shore of a saline lake.

as an oily film on the surface of the aquarium water. The molecules of these so-called surfactants are considered to be bipolar, with one end of the molecule being attracted to air and the other being attracted to water.

Anatomy of a protein skimmer

A protein skimmer is essentially a tall transparent cylindrical chamber that encloses a column of water. A large number of very tiny bubbles are produced at the bottom of the column by pumping air through an airstone (usually made of limewood) or by a motor-driven venturi valve. As the bubbles rise through the chamber, the bipolar surfactants adhere to the bubbles and are transported to the top of the chamber, where they accumulate in a thick brown foam. As the foam continues to build in volume, it spills over into a collection cup located at the top of the unit and collapses into a foul-looking brown liquid. The aquarist can then simply detach the collection cup, rinse it out in the sink, and replace it on the skimmer unit.

Airstone-driven skimmers

There are several different styles of protein skimmer available on the market, and each has its distinct advantages and disadvantages. The most basic and least costly is the airstone-driven columnar kind that is designed to be placed directly into the aquarium. This style is relatively simple to use and reasonably efficient, although you may need to repeatedly adjust the height of the skimmer chamber relative to the water surface to achieve the proper foam consistency, especially just after replacing the airstone. These skimmers are also somewhat bulky, so they may detract from the esthetics of the aquarium unless you go to great lengths to conceal the chamber behind rocks or decorations.

The most efficient form of tank-mounted protein skimmer is the counter-current style. With this type of skimmer, the water flows in through slots near the top of the chamber and travels down toward the bottom. Since the water flows in the opposite direction to the rising stream of bubbles, the contact time between water and air is maximized.

An external airstone-driven skimmer is a good alternative if you don't want a big unsightly cylinder taking up space in your aquarium. However, this type of skimmer is slightly more costly due to the fact that it must be made watertight. Also, these skimmers are, by necessity, much taller than the tank-mounted kind in order to get sufficient contact time between the rising bubbles and the water in the chamber. This means that, in some cases, the appropriate external skimmer for a larger tank would be too tall to fit beneath the aquarium in a cabinet-style stand. It's important to remember that with both the tank-mounted and external airstone-driven protein skimmers, the airstone will clog over time and must be replaced on a regular basis to ensure proper bubble size and to keep the protein skimmer operating at peak efficiency.

Venturi-driven skimmers

Unless you're operating on a very restricted budget, I would suggest that it's worth paying a few extra dollars at the outset for a venturi protein skimmer. These skimmers have several advantages over the kind that utilize airstones. For one thing, the venturi valve produces a whirling vortex–rather like a tiny tornado–within the chamber, which provides optimum

Some protein skimmers are powered by airstones.

Venturi skimmer.

Part 2

Rating the skimmers

In-tank airstone-driven skimmers	External airstone-driven skimmers
• Least costly	• Don't disrupt aquarium aesthetic
• Easy to use	• More costly than in-tank models
• Require frequent height adjustment	• Taller and harder to conceal
• Bulky and detract from aquarium aesthetic	• Airstone clogs over time
• Airstone clogs over time	
• Least efficient	

Venturi skimmers

- Produce whirling vortex of bubbles for optimum contact time between air and water
- Smaller and easier to conceal than external airstone-driven models
- No airstone to clog
- Most costly, but worth the added expense

Note: Whether driven by a venturi valve or an airstone, the most efficient skimmers have a "counter-current" design. That is, the water flows in from the top of the chamber and down toward the bottom in the opposite direction to the rising bubbles.

Live rock is often shipped wrapped in wet paper.

contact time between air and water. For this reason, venturi models can be much smaller and more easily hidden than columnar airstone-driven models, while producing better results. Also, you don't have to worry about constantly replacing clogged airstones if you decide to go with a venturi skimmer.

Live rock: Who you callin' an oxymoron?

Ask the average non-aquarist whether he or she has ever heard of live rock, and you're likely to get an expression of utter bewilderment in response. I must confess that the first time I heard an aquarium dealer mention live rock, the first thing that popped into my head was the venomous stonefish. In my defense, I was much younger then and had kept only freshwater aquariums up to that point. After all, a stonefish is living, and it does look rather like a rock, right?

But as I soon discovered, live rock is not as big an oxymoron as it might seem, and it plays a very significant role in the mini-reef aquarium.

In simple terms, live rocks are pieces of coral rubble that have broken off the reef under the influence of storms and heavy surge. As they lie in the sand around the base of the reef, they become heavily colonized by various beneficial microorganisms, a host of tiny invertebrates, pink and purple coralline algae, and certain forms of macroalgae. In other words, it's not the rocks themselves that are alive, but rather the myriad of organisms that encrust their surfaces and inhabit every crack and crevice. Live rocks also carry with them an amazing potential for future life in the form of numerous eggs, larvae, and spores, which are deposited by various means into the tiny pores of the rocks as they rest on the ocean floor.

Live rock aquaculture

The ecologically minded reader might be concerned about the sustainability of wild live rock collection and the potential for damage to the coral reefs by unscrupulous collectors. Both of these concerns are well justified, and steps are being taken in many parts of the world to encourage the practice of live rock aquaculture in order to satisfy the ever-growing demand from the aquarium industry without placing additional collection pressure on the reefs. In fact, federal law currently forbids the collection of live rock in all of the waters surrounding the continental United States. This ruling has encouraged a number of environmentally conscious entrepreneurs to set up commercial aquaculture sites around the Florida Keys and in other suitable locations.

Live rock can be easily aquacultured.

Live rock aquaculture is a relatively straightforward, albeit time-consuming, process. The operator chooses a desirable site on the ocean floor in strict accordance with governmental regulations and builds a sort of artificial reef–basically a big pile or several piles of rock–on the site. The rock pile is usually placed on top of some kind of environmentally friendly underlayment (concrete patio blocks, untreated wood lattice, etc.) to keep the lower portion of the pile from sinking into the sand. In most cases, limestone rock is used, but any highly porous, irregularly shaped rock will work just as well. Once the rock pile is in place, all the operator can do is wait for nature to take its course. Within approximately two years, unless a tropical storm or hurricane scores a direct hit on the pile (a more common occurrence than you might think), the rock is usually fully inoculated with desirable organisms and is ready to be harvested and shipped to dealers.

George scores a direct hit

To give you some appreciation of the impact hurricanes can have on live rock aquaculture projects, consider what happened when Hurricane George hit the Florida Keys. In the summer of 1997, I helped a personal friend who leases a live rock aquaculture site off Plantation Key to install 18 tons of coquina rock on the ocean floor. First we built a large "patio" out of concrete slabs to keep the rock pile from sinking into the sand. Then, under the hot Florida sun, we painstakingly lowered the rocks onto the concrete pad one small load at a time (loading the rocks and patio stones onto the boat was no picnic either, I might add).

A little over one year later, with no regard for our toil and sweat, Hurricane George passed through, swept the rock off the patio, and unceremoniously buried it in the sand—in 56 feet of water! The nerve of that hurricane! The real tragedy is, the rock pile was just starting to develop a nice coating of coralline algae and a diverse assortment of encrusting organisms. Oh well, if at first you don't succeed, try, try again.

Transporting and curing live rock

Live rock is traditionally shipped out of water, wrapped in wet newspaper, although I know of at least one operator who is developing a method for keeping the rock completely submerged from the time of collection until the time of delivery. The problem with the standard "dry" shipping method is that a certain percentage of the organisms encrusting the rocks will die off before they ever reach the dealers' tanks. Needless to say, you'd never want to place rocks covered with dead or dying organisms into an established aquarium. The resultant pollution would completely overload the biofilter and likely wipe out every animal in the tank. Instead, the rock needs to be "cured" before it can be safely introduced into the aquarium. In some instances, dealers will cure their live rock before putting it up for sale, but since this adds to the price of the rock, many will leave the curing to the customer as a cost-cutting and labor-saving measure.

Prior to curing the rocks, it's a good idea to clean them of any obviously dead or dying organisms. Carefully brush off any sediment that may still be clinging to the rocks as well as any undesirable algae or slimy, discolored patches. It's also a good idea to remove any sponges from the rocks, as they are very unlikely to survive in the aquarium, especially if they have spent any time in the open air. Some reef aquarists suggest spreading the rocks out on a waterproof tarp or plastic sheet at this stage so you can check each one out thoroughly. Just be sure to keep the rocks moist during the cleaning process by spraying them frequently with salt water. This technique may also reveal any nasty live rock "stowaways" (mantis shrimp, for example) that you don't want in your aquarium. Believe me, it's much easier to catch and destroy unwelcome pests before they find their way into your aquarium.

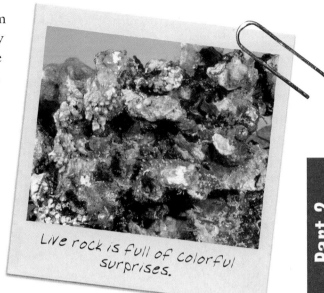

Live rock is full of colorful surprises.

The actual curing process simply involves storing the rock in a separate container filled with salt water while the aforementioned die-off process occurs. Large plastic storage tubs or even plastic garbage cans make ideal curing "vats." Numerous water changes are performed to eliminate the ammonia and nitrite produced by the decomposing organisms. The more efficiently you clean the rocks prior to curing, the shorter the actual curing time will be, but you can expect it to take somewhere in the vicinity of two weeks before the rock is ready for the aquarium. A fairly reliable way to determine whether the rock is fully cured is to perform a "sniff test." If you take a whiff of the curing vat and detect the scent of rotten eggs, you'll know that the die-off process is still taking place, and additional water changes will be necessary.

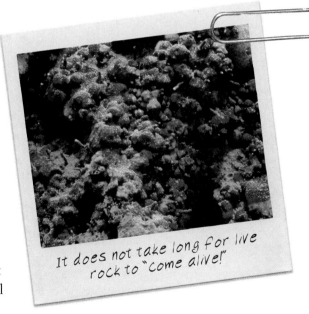

It does not take long for live rock to "come alive!"

Part 2

What do live rocks do?

In the fish-only aquarium, live rock is largely unnecessary. In fact, most of the desirable invertebrates and algae that encrust live rock would likely be gobbled up by the fish, leaving nothing but bare rock behind. There's no sense in paying the long dollar for high-quality live rock only to provide a very costly snack for your fish. However, in the mini-reef aquarium, live rock performs several very important functions. One of these functions is to serve as a physical platform to which the assorted sessile invertebrates can attach themselves. But more importantly, due to its extremely porous nature, high-quality live rock provides ample surface area for nitrifying bacteria to colonize. For this reason, many reef aquarists feel that it's redundant to add a wet-dry filter or some other commercially manufactured biofilter to a mini-reef system containing live rock. However, one could also argue that no real harm can come from having a super abundance of biological filtration.

If adequate water circulation is provided in the aquarium, live rock can also aid in the denitrification process. The same microbes that form the basis of Jaubert's plenum system can colonize the interior portions of live rock, provided the rock is sufficiently porous. A high level of porosity is necessary for two reasons. First, it allows just enough oxygen to penetrate deep into the rock to create the anoxic conditions favored by the denitrifying bacteria. Second, it provides a pathway for nitrate-rich water to reach the bacteria, which then convert the nitrate to free nitrogen gas.

The mini "cleanup crew"

Live rock also supports a large population of miniature motile invertebrates (tiny crustaceans, brittlestars, etc.) that emerge from their tiny burrows, usually at night, and scavenge through the rockwork and substrate for anything remotely resembling food. Some will even glean whatever

Two dragonets with an affinity for live rock

If you're looking for some beautiful inoffensive fish to keep in your mini-reef, you can't go wrong with either the mandarinfish (*Synchiropus splendidus*) or the psychedelic fish (*Synchiropus picturatus*). Both have wildly exotic coloration and patterning, and both are extraordinarily well behaved around sessile invertebrates. Ironically, it wasn't until aquarists started keeping mini-reefs full of live rock that these two fish could even be kept alive with any success in captivity. It turns out their diet consists primarily of the tiny creatures that inhabit live rock, including amphipods, copepods, mysis shrimp, and protozoans.

scant nutrients they can derive from the waste material of the larger organisms in the aquarium. As a result of the efforts of this miniature "cleanup crew," the aquarium water remains remarkably low in nutrients, which is very similar to the water conditions on a natural coral reef and very desirable for sensitive corals and other sessile invertebrates.

Berlin system

In the previous chapter, we examined the process of Natural Nitrate Reduction using a plenum. But the natural approach to maintaining a reef aquarium is not limited to Jaubert's technique. Another method, known as the Berlin method (conceived in Germany during the 1970s), relies heavily on the use of live rock and live sand to carry out the important processes of biological filtration and denitrification. With this approach, no plenum is used, and the only additional filtering device used is a high-quality protein skimmer, which eliminates dissolved organic compounds. Since such systems seldom include fish, there is very little particulate matter to contend with, which makes mechanical filtration largely unnecessary. Any debris that does make its way into the aquarium can be vacuumed out easily during routine partial water changes.

Live sand

We've already discussed live rock and how it contributes to nitrification and denitrification, but what is the role of live sand in the Berlin system? As was mentioned in the previous chapter, live sand is sand harvested from the ocean floor that contains an array of tiny creatures, ranging from beneficial microorganisms to sand-sifting

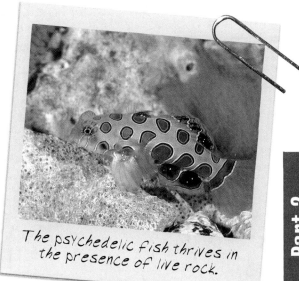

The psychedelic fish thrives in the presence of live rock.

All live sand is not created equal.

Part 2

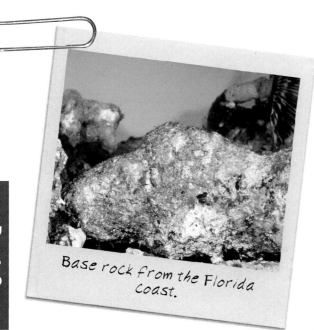

Base rock from the Florida coast.

Beneficial colonies will grow on mined rock in time.

crustaceans and echinoderms. When the proper depth of sand is used (approximately 2-3 inches) in the aquarium, anoxic conditions favorable to denitrifying bacteria tend to prevail deep within the sand. The sand-sifting creatures continually turn the top layer of the sand over, thereby guaranteeing the proper oxygen gradient throughout the sand. Without these creatures, the sand would eventually compact and become anaerobic, which would undermine the denitrification process.

Not all live rock (or live sand) is created equal

It's important to keep in mind that spending time on the ocean floor is not the only criterion necessary for rock or sand to be considered "live" and therefore suitable for aquarium use. Remember, you're looking for a full complement of beneficial encrusting organisms, not just a batch of very costly "base rock." On several occasions, I have seen bargain "live rocks" for sale that had not a single organism visible on their surfaces. Perhaps such rocks would suffice for aquascaping a fish-only aquarium, but they would be grossly inadequate for a mini-reef—especially one that relies exclusively on natural filtration. If all you're after are rocks to be used for aquascaping purposes, you can easily get by using inexpensive terrestrially mined limestone, tufa, or lava rock. Even though these rocks will be essentially devoid of life when you buy them, they will in time support colonies of beneficial nitrifying bacteria and provide ample hiding places for the fish in your aquarium. You must of course avoid the use of rocks that could leach harmful chemicals into the water.

The particular site on the ocean floor from which live rock or live sand has been harvested can also have an impact on quality. If collected from areas within close proximity to shore, there's a strong probability that the rock or sand will contain various harmful pollutants resulting from boat traffic, the discharge of sewage, chemical runoff from farmers' fields, and a host of other sources. Live sand from such areas has also been known to harbor—in addition to the pollutants listed above—disease-causing microbes that can wreak havoc on your valued aquarium specimens. Reef aquarists must be especially wary of live sand collected close to shore, as it is a known source of the *Vibrio* virus, which is a major killer of small polyp stony corals in the aquarium.

So how can you be sure that you're getting the best quality live rock or live sand possible? Actually, there's no way to be 100-percent sure, but buying from a reputable dealer is certainly a step in the right direction. And don't be afraid to ask questions about the source of the rock or sand, the manner

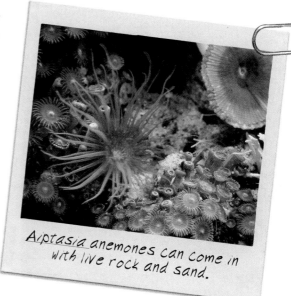

Aiptasia anemones can come in with live rock and sand.

in which it was collected, and the way it was handled after collection. A trustworthy dealer should be able to answer most, if not all, of these questions. More importantly, you should trust your own senses when selecting live rock or sand. If a particular dealer is offering "discount" live rock with no visible signs of life, or live sand that is coated with cyanobacteria (a.k.a. slime algae, or blue-green algae), you might want to take your business elsewhere.

Beware of rocks bearing pests!

Thus far in our discussion of live rock I've made repeated allusions to "beneficial encrusting organisms." However, as I briefly indicated in the section about cleaning and curing the rock, there are several organisms that have been known to stow away on live rock that can become quite troublesome within the confines of an aquarium. Some of the more irksome pests that fall into this category include mantis shrimps, fireworms, and *Aiptasia* anemones. Unfortunately for aquarists, some of these organisms may arrive in the form of unhatched eggs or tiny larvae obscured within the pores of the rock, so they may escape detection during the processes of cleaning and curing.

Mantis shrimp are tough cookies.

Fireworms are nasty, but they can be controlled.

Thumb-splitting shrimp

Some of the more volatile of the live rock stowaways are the mantis shrimp, known by fishermen and live rock collectors as "thumbsplitters." Mantis shrimp are so named because of their large stalked eyes, elongated bodies, and hooked feeding appendages (chelae), which make them look for all intents and purposes like terrestrial praying mantises. They get the "thumbsplitter" nickname from their propensity to lash out with lightning speed at prey items and predators with their formidable chelae. When accidentally disturbed or handled by unwary aquarists, they can deliver a painful puncture wound.

Mantis shrimp are extremely efficient predators of fish, some sessile invertebrates, and other crustaceans, so securing a meal in a well-stocked aquarium is rather like "shooting fish in a barrel" for them. Also, since they are primarily nocturnal feeders, aquarists are often unaware of their presence until prized specimens start to disappear. Unfortunately, most mantis shrimp remain hidden within holes in the live rock during the day, so locating and eradicating them can be problematic. Some suggest that you can trap a mantis shrimp by placing a baited hamster maze into the aquarium. The theory is that the shrimp will be lured into the "labyrinth" by the scent of the bait, but it will be unable to find its way back out.

That being said, I should mention that not all mantis shrimp are equally harmful in the aquarium, and catching sight of one of these critters is not necessarily cause to tear the aquarium apart in order to effect a capture. In fact, some of the larger mantis shrimp species are rather exquisitely colored, which makes them attractive to certain hobbyists who have a penchant for unusual marine species. Of course, given their predatory nature, it is necessary to give these "thumbsplitters" an aquarium all to themselves.

Don't get burned by fireworms

Another live rock stowaway that can wreak havoc in the mini-reef aquarium is *Hermodice carunculata,* one of the polychaete worms of the family Amphinomidae, generally called fireworms because of the venomous nature of the bristles covering their bodies. Fireworms are easily identified by the rows of fuzzy-looking bristles along their sides. But don't be fooled! Those fuzzy bristles are actually needle-like spines that can inflict a painful sting–even if the aquarist makes contact by accident. The sensation produced by the sting is similar to that of being burned by fire.

Fireworms and other polychaetes typically scavenge for detritus in the substrate, but *H. carunculata* will also feed on gorgonian polyps and other invertebrates. Like the mantis shrimps, fireworms can be very evasive and difficult to capture. However, there are commercially manufactured traps available on the market that can be very effective in eradicating these pests. There are also certain fish, including triggerfish and tilefish, that will happily devour any fireworms unfortunate enough to cross their paths. However, introducing either of these fish to a mini-reef aquarium for the purpose of bristleworm control would be counterproductive, since they enjoy nibbling on certain cnidarian polyps as much as *H. carunculata* does.

Chelmon rostratus is well equipped to dig out aiptasia.

Some anemones you don't want in your mini-reef

Much to the dismay of many reef aquarists, some of the most desirable anemone species are notoriously difficult to keep alive in the mini-reef aquarium because of their exacting water quality and lighting requirements. On the other hand, there is one group of anemones that not only thrives under less than ideal conditions but also resists almost any effort to eliminate them from the aquarium. These are the *Aiptasia* anemones, also called rock anemones, or glass anemones, which usually make their way into the aquarium concealed within the pores of live rock.

Aiptasia are small drab brown or green anemones that can spread like wildfire throughout a mini-reef aquarium if left to their own devices. Now, you might be asking yourself, what's so bad about anemones that are easy to care for and propagate? Isn't that the perfect type of organism for the reef aquarium? Well, if aiptasia were attractive and kept their tentacles to themselves, that would be true, but unfortunately, they aren't, and they don't. That is to say, aiptasia add nothing to the mini-reef in terms of esthetics, and they have a nasty habit of repeatedly stinging desirable invertebrates, occasionally to the point of death, in order to make room for themselves among the rocks.

Death by lethal injection

Aiptasia are nearly impossible to kill through mechanical means. Any attempt to cut them off the rock merely prompts them to withdraw back into their holes out of reach.

Death to aiptasia, by injection.

Even if you're quick enough to cut away a portion of one of these animals, it will merely regrow as if nothing happened. These troublesome anemones can be eliminated by injecting each individual animal with potassium chloride, but this is an extremely tedious and painstaking process that often must be done repeatedly in order to be effective. Some also suggest injecting a mixture of calcium hydroxide and water (so-called kalkwasser) as an alternative to potassium chloride.

Animals that eat aiptasia

If you'd rather not fool around with needles and chemicals, you might want to try introducing one of the animals known to feed on aiptasia in the wild. One of these is the copperband butterflyfish (*Chelmon rostratus*), which has been used successfully by many reef aquarists to eradicate aiptasia. Unfortunately, this fish's taste for invertebrate flesh doesn't necessarily end with aiptasia, and it may expand its menu to include your prized specimens. In addition, it can be very difficult to net and

Live rock stowaways: the lineup of usual suspects

Suspect:	Wanted for:	Controls:
Mantis shrimp (alias "thumbsplitter")	Devouring tankmates and wounding aquarists	Search and destroy
Fireworm	Devouring tankmates and stinging aquarists	Commercial traps
Aiptasia anemone (alias glass anemone)	Nettling neighbors	Potassiuim chloride injection Kalkwasser injection Copperband butterflyfish Red-legged hermit crab

remove a butterflyfish from a mini-reef aquarium if things don't go as planned. A better choice of predator might be the red-legged hermit crab (*Dardanus megistos*), which will greedily devour *Aiptasia* while being completely inoffensive to the other invertebrates in the aquarium.

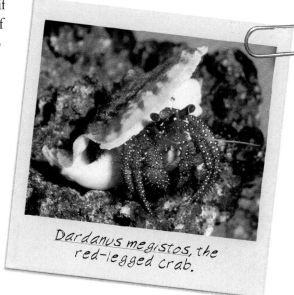

Dardanus megistos, the red-legged crab.

Water Changes: The Ultimate Key to Aquarium Success

Up to this point, we've examined several methods of filtering and purifying the water in your aquarium, each of which relies heavily on specialized equipment or certain biological processes within the aquarium system. But in this chapter, we'll discuss the critical role that routine partial water changes play in the management of healthy, thriving marine fish and/or invertebrates.

The water change is, arguably, the most important of all maintenance tasks carried out by the aquarist. In fact, I would suggest that no amount of expensive, high-tech filtering gadgets and gizmos can completely eliminate the need for water changes, although there are some who would disagree with this assessment. The beauty of water changes is that

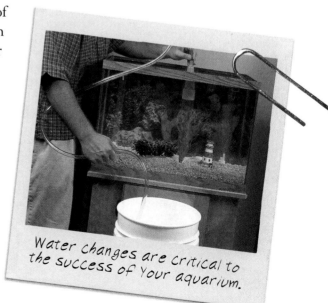

Water changes are critical to the success of your aquarium.

Tricky triggerfish!

I'll Huff, and I'll Puff

The various triggerfish of the Balistidae family have an unusual way of devouring sea urchins, seastars, and other spiny echinoderms without injuring themselves in the process. First they blow them over onto their backs with a forceful puff of water from their mouths. Once the "business end" of the prey item is rendered harmless, they "go to town" on the soft underparts with their impressive dentition.

they are completely within the control of the aquarist, and to a certain extent, they serve as a safeguard against a wide range of water-quality blunders common to novice aquarists (and quite a few experienced ones, I might add), such as overfeeding and overstocking.

Changing times

In the "good old days" of the marine aquarium hobby–before the benefits of water changes were fully understood and before low-cost, high-quality synthetic sea salt mixes had arrived on the market–water changes were generally postponed for as long as possible. In fact, utilizing the same aquarium water for a prolonged period of time was considered to be a bragging point by many pioneer hobbyists. And who could blame them? If I had to concoct my own salt mix out of various chemical elements or make repeated trips to the beach to collect buckets of natural sea water, I probably wouldn't bother with water changes either. But nowadays, modern one-step salt mixes make it extremely easy, and relatively inexpensive, for marine aquarists to give their charges all the clean salt water they need.

Guaranteed nitrate reduction

Of all the methods of nitrate reduction available to aquarists, the only 100-percent guaranteed method is the water change. It's also the safest. There is really no downside to changing the water unless it is done so frequently that the fish are kept in a constant state of heightened arousal. But if a predictable water change schedule is put in place immediately after the aquarium's biological filter becomes fully established, the nitrates and other undesirable compounds should remain at a constant low level.

I should mention, however, that in some cases nitrate might be present in tap water, which means you could be adding low levels of nitrate to the aquarium with each water change. With a fish-only aquarium, the amount of nitrate added in this way would be inconsequential, but it could make a difference in a mini-reef where little or no measurable nitrate should be present. To safeguard against this eventuality—or if a call to your local water utility reveals that nitrate is indeed present in your municipal water supply—you might want to process your tap water through a reverse-osmosis unit (a good idea anyway, but more on that later) or a denitrifying filter before mixing in the salt and adding it to the aquarium.

Phosphate reduction

Phosphate is another dissolved compound that can accumulate to harmful levels if not diluted through regular partial water changes. Phosphate is a compound containing phosphorus and oxygen that is present in all living things. It is usually introduced into the aquarium with fish foods, as a result of various biological processes, or via low-quality synthetic salt mixes. Like nitrate, phosphate can also be found in tap water. In the aquarium, high levels of phosphate can fuel blooms of filamentous algae and unsightly cyanobacteria (slime algae, or blue-green algae). Fish are not especially troubled by phosphate, but invertebrates respond poorly to even miniscule amounts. Stony corals are especially sensitive to phosphate, as it interferes with their ability to manufacture their calcareous "skeletons."

Detecting phosphate is relatively easy, since it typically makes its presence known by the proliferation of algae. You can also test for it with a phosphate test kit available at any aquarium store. On the other hand, eliminating phosphate altogether can be a much

An Underwater Odd Couple

The various shrimp gobies, which are members of approximately five different genera in the enormous Gobiidae family, get their name from the peculiar mutualistic relationship that they develop with pistol shrimps (family Alpheidae). With each shrimp/goby team, the shrimp uses its outstanding digging skills to maintain the tunnel that both occupy, and it won't hesitate to drive off intruders with an audible snap from its impressive claws. Fortunately (for the goby), it will never turn its claws against its goby companion. The pistol shrimp also benefits from the relationship because the goby stands guard for predators as the shrimp cleans the burrow or sifts the sand for food. The only question is, can two completely unrelated marine organisms occupy the same burrow without driving each other crazy?

Part 2

trickier proposition, since it can arrive in the aquarium through so many different sources. If your water supply is the suspected or confirmed (by testing) source of phosphate, you can usually take care of the problem by filtering your tap water through a reverse osmosis unit. You should also check the package of your synthetic sea salt mix to make sure it contains no phosphate. With high-quality mixes, this information should be clearly emblazoned on the package. If neither your tap water nor your salt mix is the culprit, you may need to cut back on the amount you're feeding or reduce the number of specimens in the aquarium. Of course, stepping up your water change regimen is the most efficient way to keep phosphate levels under control.

The effect of water changes on aquarium livestock

In order to truly understand the importance of water changes for your fish and invertebrates, try to imagine being locked in a poorly ventilated room for a month with several of your closest friends. Assume that you'll still be given three square meals each day and possibly television privileges, but no one will be allowed to leave the confines of the room. Under such circumstances, everyone's nerves might get a little frayed, but it would, perhaps, be tolerable. Now imagine being confined to that same poorly ventilated room, but with no functional plumbing and no provision for garbage removal. Now things are getting a bit dicey! Within a matter of days, everyone in the room would likely be pleading with their captors (Just for the sake of illustration, let's assume they're giant fish, keeping humans as pets.) for a window or door to be opened to allow for at least a partial exchange of air. That's essentially what we put our fish and invertebrates through when we put off water changes for a prolonged period of time. Sure, the aquarium's filtration system can eliminate many of the pollutants, but ultimately, harmful compounds will accumulate until they reach intolerable levels.

We can never exactly duplicate natural seawater.

It's not surprising, then, that both fish and invertebrates exhibit much better overall health,

Avoid "gadget overload"

The marine aquarium hobby is rife with high-tech equipment and gadgets, many of which you can live without when you're just getting started, especially if you decide to go with a fish-only aquarium. For example, as you start shopping for equipment you'll probably hear about devices like ozone generators, ultraviolet sterilizers, calcium reactors, and ion exchangers. And that's just a small sampling! While each of these devices can play an important role in your overall water quality and the health of the specimens in your aquarium, they simply aren't necessary for a basic system. Besides, all of these "bells and whistles" can really take a bite out of your aquarium budget. You'll be much happier in the long run if you start out with just the basic equipment and add devices as your confidence grows and your budget allows.

Part 2

superior coloration, and a heightened level of activity after a partial water change is performed. In fact, after observing the almost joyful response of my fish to a long overdue water change, I often have to wonder why I don't perform them more frequently.

How much and how often?

In most cases, frequent smaller water changes are preferable to infrequent larger ones. A good rule of thumb is to change approximately 10 percent of the tank volume every two weeks, although some busy aquarists favor a 20-percent water change once a month. In a larger system containing very few specimens, a monthly water change might be adequate, but I would strongly encourage biweekly changes—especially while you're still getting accustomed to the ins and outs of your new aquarium. Remember, the conditions on tropical coral reefs are highly stable, and changing the water more often ensures that the water parameters will not fluctuate markedly. Frequent changes also ensure that the various trace elements found in synthetic salt mixes, which are necessary for the healthy functioning of marine fish and invertebrates, are replenished in a timely manner.

It is good to clean the glass as slime harbors bacteria.

Clean impellers on filters and powerheads regularly.

Sometimes bigger is better

There are certain events that might demand a very large water change, such as a sudden precipitous rise in ammonia or nitrite levels. However, in a case like this, you can't just change the water and "call it a day." The spiking ammonia or nitrite would most likely be a symptom of some major problem in the system, such as a dead, decomposing animal hidden in the rockwork or a broken down filter. Whatever the source of the problem, you would need to locate and correct it with dispatch.

Occasionally, you might want to perform larger water changes in order to keep your aquarium's nitrate level within the acceptable range. Even when performing routine 10-percent water changes, the nitrate level can rise very gradually over time, depending on the biological load in the aquarium. For example, if the nitrate level in a fish-only system measures 40ppm (the approximate upper limit for most marine fish) prior to a 10-percent water change, it would only be reduced by 4ppm following the change. In other words, the nitrate level would only be diluted to

Nature abhors a vacuum—but remoras don't!

One of the more unusual adaptations exhibited by a marine fish is the suction disk located atop the flattened head of the remora (family Echeneidae). The remora comes by its nickname, "shark sucker," honestly. Its first dorsal fin is modified into a disk that is covered with a series of ridges—actually modified dorsal spines. When a suitable "chauffer" swims by, the remora glides beneath it and attaches its disk to the underside of the shark (or turtle, or whale, or boat—they're not picky!) through a series of muscle contractions, forming an almost unbreakable vacuum seal. Contrary to popular belief, remoras do not clean parasites from the bodies of their hosts. Rather, they use their hosts to get where they want to go and will detach to hunt for themselves whenever suitable prey items are spotted.

approximately 36ppm, which is still dangerously close to exceeding the safe range. If more specimens are added following that water change, or if the aquarist overfeeds the fish on several occasions, the nitrate level could rise well beyond the safe level before the next scheduled water change, and changing only 10 percent of the water volume might not be adequate to bring the nitrate level back into the safe range.

A step-by-step water change

Performing a routine partial water change is a fairly straightforward proposition, but it won't hurt for us to examine the process in detail anyway. When I first got started in the marine aquarium hobby, I found it extremely helpful to work from a checklist whenever I did a water change. That way, I could be sure that I hadn't missed any important steps. I also included several additional maintenance tasks in my water change checklist to ensure that they would be completed in a timely manner. The list looked something like this:

Long-handled implements are excellent for larger tanks.

• Disconnect power to filters and pumps.

• Remove and clean cover glass.

• Clean algae from the front glass pane with an algae magnet (I allow it to grow on the sides and back as "tang fodder.")

• Siphon 10 percent (or more if desired) of water volume into bucket/vacuum substrate.

• Rinse out prefilters and filter media, using aquarium water in bucket.

• Clean patches of slime algae from rockwork.

• Inspect all equipment for proper functioning.

• Clean and rinse protein skimmer, filters, pumps, hoses, and attachments using assorted brushes and aquarium water.

• Clean "salt creep" from power cords, top edge of the aquarium, etc.

• Mix new salt water, using dechlorinated tap water processed through reverse-osmosis and a high-quality salt mix.

• Make sure the temperature and salinity of the replacement water match that of the aquarium water.

• Very gradually add the replacement water to the aquarium.

• Power up the equipment and replace the cover glass.

Diatom filters do a good job of polishing the water.

Of course, there's no law that says you have to follow this list exactly as I've outlined it. You can modify it in any way that makes sense to you. Of course, if you're not as forgetful as I am, there's no need to make a list at all.

You may also have noticed that I didn't mention anything about replacing filter media on the checklist. That's because it's best to change filter media a couple of days before or after a water change so you don't disrupt the biological filter too much. Remember, nitrifying bacteria will proliferate on any suitable surface in the aquarium, including the sponge or floss in your mechanical filter and any activated carbon that you might be using in the system. If all of these media are removed from the aquarium simultaneously, you may be eliminating a substantial portion of your biofilter, which could precipitate a dangerous spike in ammonia or nitrite.

How to avoid a mouthful of dirty salt water

One aspect of water changes that literally leaves a bad taste in many aquarists' mouths is having to get the siphon started by placing one end of the hose in the aquarium and sucking on the other end. Those who don't react quickly enough once the water starts flowing usually receive a mouthful of dirty salt water for their trouble. While this is not likely to result in any major health problems, it's certainly not a pleasant experience!

Fortunately, there's a technique that you can use to start the siphon without ever putting the hose to your lips. In order for this method to work, the bucket used to catch the wastewater must be positioned well below the level of the aquarium, but not so low that the hose can't reach. All you have to do is place one end of the siphon hose inside the bucket, and hold the end with the wide vacuum attachment over the aquarium with the opening facing up. Slowly submerge the vacuum attachment into the aquarium water until it is completely filled with water. Then, raise the vacuum end out of the aquarium, allowing the water to rush down into the bucket. Just before all of the water drains from the vacuum end, submerge it into the aquarium again in the same fashion as before. If you time it right, the water will continue to flow into the bucket. You can then position the vacuum so that the opening faces the bottom of the aquarium and begin vacuuming the substrate. Don't be concerned if it takes you a few tries to get the hang of this method, but rest assured, once you've mastered this method, you'll never want to go back to siphoning by mouth.

Tool-wielding crustaceans

Scientists typically associate the use of tools with humans and other higher primates. But the miniscule boxer crab (*Lybia tessellata*), a mere crustacean, has been known to carry a tiny anemone in each claw and to brandish them threateningly as a warning to potential predators. To the casual observer, this is an absurd spectacle, looking rather like a crabby cheerleader with miniature pompoms, but to the crab, the anemones can mean the difference between life and death. In fact, the only time the boxing crab puts aside its tentacled weapons is when it's preparing to shed its exoskeleton.

This boxer crab is armed and dangerous.

Getting the Aquarium Up and Running

Now that we've explored the major "life support systems" for your new marine aquarium, it's time to put all the pieces together. After testing for leaks (by filling the tank with fresh water and examining the seams over a 24-hour period), your tank should be completely drained, placed on its stand and carefully leveled. Be sure to leave adequate space at the back and sides for cords, tubing, and any equipment to be added later on. Also, all of your heating, lighting, and filtration equipment should be in place and ready to be turned on when the time comes. Soon you'll be ready to start mixing salt water! But before you can begin filling the tank, you'll need to install your substrate, rockwork, and decorations (if you choose to include any), making sure that everything is firmly affixed so

Keep the tank on the level.

nothing can tumble over and crack the glass or scratch the acrylic. Believe me, you'll be surprised at how efficiently some fish and invertebrates can upset seemingly stable piles of rock with their machinations.

Suitable substrates

Using a substrate in a marine aquarium has its advantages and disadvantages. I prefer to use one for purely esthetic reasons. That is, it creates the natural look I've grown accustomed to seeing when diving on coral reefs. An appropriate substrate also has the benefit of buffering the pH of the water. In other words, substrates suitable for use in salt water will continually leach calcium carbonate, which stabilizes the pH within the desired range of 8.2 to 8.4. A substrate is also desirable if you intend to keep burrowing or sand-sifting organisms in the aquarium.

However, some would argue, especially those reef aquarists who don't favor natural filtration methods, that the substrate merely serves to entrap particulate waste, which causes the nitrate level to rise as it decomposes. The bottom line is, the decision whether or not to use a substrate is entirely up to you. As long as you're prepared to vacuum it gently during each partial water change, you shouldn't experience any water quality problems associated with the substrate.

So which materials are suitable for use as marine aquarium substrates and which are not? The best choices include crushed coral, dolomite, and aragonite gravel. Not only are these materials excellent pH buffers, but they also offer that pristine natural appearance that makes the aquarium look like an authentic "slice of coral reef." Fine-grain sand can also be used as a substrate, provided you're not using an undergravel filter. The fine grains would tend to clog the filter and reduce its effectiveness. If you decide to use sand, it's very important to turn it over occasionally to keep it from becoming anaerobic and to keep particulate matter from getting trapped. Anaerobic conditions coupled with decomposing

Goby or Blenny?

To the untrained eye, gobies (of the family Gobiidae) and blennies (of the family Blenniidae) are very difficult to tell apart. They each have similarly elongated bodies with blunt heads and large, high-set eyes, and both are primarily bottom dwellers. So how can you distinguish between the two families of fish? Blennies have small, bristle-like appendages, called cirrhi, above their eyes, which are not found on gobies. Blennies also have a single, elongated dorsal fin, whereas gobies have two distinct dorsal fins. You can also tell them apart by their respective pelvic fins. On blennies they are separate, while on gobies, they are often fused together to form a suction disc, which enables them to get a firm "finhold" on the rocky substrates that they inhabit. Finally, blennies have lateral lines, while they are absent or reduced on gobies.

waste can lead to the production of hydrogen sulfide gas, which, as you are now aware, is highly toxic to marine organisms. This is not such an issue when live sand is used because the sand-sifting organisms that inhabit the sand will turn it over continually through their feeding activities.

No brightly colored gravel, please!

The variously colored gravels that are popular in the freshwater side of the hobby are not designed for use in marine aquariums. Not only do they lack the buffering capacity of marine-grade substrates, but they also create the wrong esthetic impression. The earth-toned gravels that are most commonly used in freshwater tanks create a look more reminiscent of a riverbed or lake bottom rather than the ocean floor. As far as those garish, fluorescent-colored gravels are concerned, there may actually be laws against their use on the books somewhere, probably under the heading, "Crimes Against the Senses."

Substrate depth

In the fish-only aquarium, a substrate depth of 2 to 3 inches is generally more than adequate, and there's certainly nothing wrong with using less. The only reason you might want to make the substrate deeper is if you intend to keep certain burrowing fish, such as the different species of jawfish (family Opistognathidae), which require enough sand or gravel to completely conceal their elongated bodies while "tail-standing" in a vertical position. But if no burrowing or tunneling fish are present, the substrate is primarily decorative in purpose, and the depth is fairly arbitrary, although it will, in due time, contribute to the biological filtration of the aquarium.

The substrate should look natural.

Lawnmower blenny. The cirrhi are seen above the eye.

Everything that goes into the tank must be clean.

Make sure any adhesives used for decorating are aquarium-safe.

In my 55-gallon fish-only system, I placed approximately 1 inch of aragonite gravel in front of the rockwork, while leaving the area beneath and behind the rocks empty. This way, detritus cannot accumulate as easily in those hard-to-reach areas, and I can readily vacuum up any debris that collects at the front of the aquarium. I originally attached a powerhead on the back glass near the bottom, with its discharge directed along the back of the aquarium, to keep solid waste from settling behind the rocks. However, I have since removed it because it seemed to be an unsettling influence on the fish. It was also responsible for the death of a banded coral shrimp, which got stuck on the intake and was unable to break free. You live and learn!

Rinsing the substrate

Whichever type of substrate you choose, be sure to rinse it out thoroughly in clean fresh water to eliminate most of the fine dust that is invariably packaged along with the gravel before placing it in the aquarium. To accomplish this, simply place the gravel in a clean plastic bucket, and add water to the bucket until it rises well past the level of the gravel. Then, swirl your hand through the gravel repeatedly, and drain off the dirty water. Take care not to dump any of the substrate in the process. Repeat these steps until the water remains relatively clear. Depending on how much you buy, it may be necessary to divide the gravel into small, manageable quantities for cleaning. If you fail to rinse the substrate ahead of time, your aquarium water will assume the color of milk for several days until the dust completely settles out. Of course, live sand requires no rinsing and should never be treated in this manner.

Choosing the rockwork

Once you've settled on an appropriate substrate, you'll want to select an assortment of rocks to be fashioned into an artificial reef wall for a fish-only system or used as a foundation for the live rock in a mini-reef. Some of the better choices include tufa, limestone, coquina, and lava rock, each of which is adequately porous to promote the proliferation of nitrifying bacteria and to minimize the displacement of water. These rocks are generally soft enough so that their shapes can be altered as needed through mechanical means. Try to choose uniquely shaped rocks that can be stacked in a natural presentation without creating the look of a contrived stone wall.

Installing the rockwork

In order to ensure the stability of the rockwork in the aquarium, it should be installed on top of the bare glass bottom prior to installation of the substrate. An exception is live rock, which should be placed in the tank once it is partially filled with water. It's highly recommended that the rocks be secured to the bottom of the tank and to each other with dabs of aquarium-safe silicone to minimize the likelihood of mini-avalanches.

Some aquarists prefer to stack the rocks right up against the back pane of the aquarium to achieve maximum support and to gain the greatest amount of space at the front of the tank. And, indeed, this

Rockwork that isn't made of rock

A new, highly innovative product has recently hit the market that may eventually change the face of aquascaping as we know it, artificial "rocks" made of ceramic or glass foam. These foam rocks are very lightweight, extremely porous, displace very little water, and they offer an incredible amount of surface area for nitrifying bacteria to colonize. These features make them ideal for biological filtration in both freshwater and marine aquariums. In fact, chunks of the foam can be placed in filtration devices as bio-filter media. The foam rocks can also be cut easily to create nooks, crannies, and caves for fish to hide in or simply to get them to fit into the desired space.

The fish often use the space behind the rocks.

is the best technique to employ in a mini-reef if you want to display the invertebrates to their greatest advantage. However, in a fish-only aquarium, it is desirable to leave a gap between the back glass and the rockwork so the fish have plenty of room to hide. Although it seems counterintuitive, they'll actually spend more time out in the open if they know that ample refuge is close at hand (fin?). Leaving a gap at the back and on either side of the rockwork also creates a nice circular swimming pattern, so the fish don't have to reverse direction continually as they move about the tank. The open space at the back of the tank also makes it easier to conceal submersible heaters, undergravel filter uplift tubes, filter return hoses, and any equipment that must be placed directly into the main aquarium.

Another important factor to consider when arranging the rockwork is the number of caves, crevices, nooks, and crannies that are provided for the fish. Again, the more hiding places and "bolt holes" you provide, the more safe and secure the fish will feel, and the more they'll make themselves available for your viewing pleasure at the front of the tank. If you select irregularly shaped rocks rather than uniform, slab-shaped ones, you'll be able to create a "honeycomb" effect, similar to what the fish would find in their natural surroundings on the coral reef. This "honeycomb" layout also makes it easier for the invertebrates in a mini-reef aquarium to find suitable ledges and outcroppings on which to secure a foothold.

Glass foam filter materials and decorations are sound choices for saltwater applications.

Are decorations redundant?

The decision whether or not to include decorations in a marine aquarium is largely based on personal preference and esthetic sensibility. Some would suggest that tropical marine fish and invertebrates are so strikingly beautiful that there's little need for additional accents in the aquarium. Others feel that "aquascaping" with a few tasteful and judiciously placed decorations only serves to enhance the natural beauty of the marine organisms. If you fall into the latter category, by all means, feel free to experiment with a few decorative elements. Just be sure that any ornament you're thinking of placing in the aquarium, whether it's natural or artificial, is completely safe for use in a marine aquarium.

Play it safe when you decorate

Some of the more whimsical decorations that are commonly sold for freshwater aquariums, you know, those plastic deep-sea divers, sunken ships, skeletons, treasure chests, castles, and the like, may not be suitable for use in marine aquariums. In some instances, they may even contain paints or other materials that will release toxins when they come into contact with salt water. To play it safe, check the label of any artificial aquarium decoration to verify that it is specifically manufactured for use in salt water, and if there is any question, don't risk it. As a general rule, you can immediately disqualify any decorations that contain metals, since the metal may react with the salt water and begin to rust.

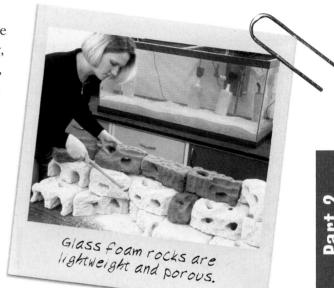

Glass foam rocks are lightweight and porous.

Even better than the real thing!

Some of the better decorative choices for marine fish-only aquariums are the synthetic reproductions of sessile invertebrates, such as stony corals, sponges, and sea fans, that are manufactured out of environmentally friendly resins. Compared to similar products of the past, which were rather garishly colored and clumsily fashioned, the modern versions are painted in naturalistic tones and are very intricately and convincingly designed. Once these products spend a little time in the aquarium and begin to develop a natural patina of algae, it can be hard to tell them apart from the real thing.

The trouble with coral skeletons

In the early days of marine fishkeeping, no aquarium was complete without at least a few bleached coral skeletons. At that time, they provided the only means of creating a naturalistic reef setting apart from keeping live sessile invertebrates. Nowadays, the popularity of using natural coral skeletons as decorations is beginning to wane among aquarists for several reasons.

For one thing, the wild collection of coral skeletons can have a serious impact on the health and sustainability of the reefs, depending on the particular collection method that is used. For another, the heavily convoluted skeletons, which are usually considered the

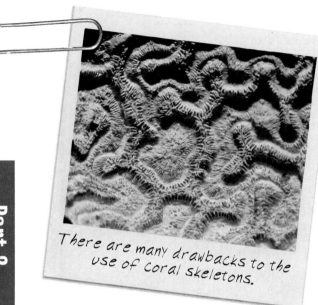

There are many drawbacks to the use of coral skeletons.

Reverse osmosis unit.

most attractive, can be difficult to clean thoroughly. This means decaying polyps may be introduced into the aquarium where they will continue to decompose to the detriment of water quality. Finally, coral skeletons tend to trap uneaten food, fish waste, and other detritus with remarkable efficiency, again, leading to the degradation of water quality. Large univalve seashells are also big detritus trappers. Though some shells are extremely beautiful and great fun to collect, your best bet is to leave them out of your aquarium unless they serve as alternate homes for a resident hermit crab.

Time to get wet!

Now that your substrate, rockwork, and decorations are in place (with the possible exceptions of the live rock and live sand, which should be added after the tank has been partially filled with water), and all your heating, lighting, and water purification equipment is installed and ready for operation, it's time to mix up your first batch of salt water. However, you should be aware that your municipal tapwater supply might contain various contaminants, such as nitrate, phosphate, copper, lead, and aluminum among other things, that may be hazardous to marine life, even if they are of little consequence to humans. Also, tap water is usually treated with a chemical like chlorine or chloramine to make it safe for human consumption.

In order to ensure that no harmful contaminants or dissolved organic compounds are introduced into your aquarium, it is highly recommended that you purify your tap water with a reverse osmosis (RO) unit prior to adding the synthetic salt mix, especially if you intend to set up a mini-reef. You must also remove the chlorine or chloramine from the water with some sort of chemical dechlorinator before it is suitable for aquarium use. Dechlorinating products are very inexpensive and simple to use. Usually adding a drop or two per gallon of water is all that is necessary.

What is reverse osmosis?

The process of reverse osmosis involves forcing the water from your tap through a semi-permeable membrane that retains most of the contaminants that might either poison marine organisms directly or contribute to the overall degradation of water quality. To a certain extent, the RO membrane even excludes bacteria and viruses, although this is no guarantee that certain aquatic diseases won't be a problem. Pathogenic microorganisms can still make their way into the aquarium whenever new fish or invertebrates are introduced.

RO purified water should be used every time you prepare replacement salt water to be used after a partial water change and every time you replace fresh water lost to evaporation. Fresh water, rather than salt water, is used to compensate for evaporation because the salt that is mixed with the water does not evaporate, only pure, fresh water evaporates. If you were to "top off" the evaporated water with salt water each time, the salinity would gradually rise beyond the desired level.

Mixing the salt water

Adding the synthetic salt mix to the RO-purified and dechlorinated water is a simple procedure. Considering the significant volume of saltwater that is needed to completely fill a large aquarium, you might find it easier to mix the fresh tap water and synthetic salt in the tank itself during the initial setup phase. Of course, if you prefer, you can also mix up the salt water in separate buckets and then carefully pour it into the aquarium one bucket at a time. Once the aquarium is operating, and the fish and/or invertebrates have been added, you'll need to mix all of your salt water for partial water changes in separate buckets.

You can mix the saltwater in the tank the first time you fill it.

A hydrometer is essential.

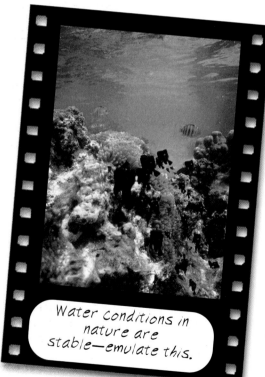

Water conditions in nature are stable—emulate this.

Be sure any buckets you use are made of plastic (preferably food-grade) and have never been contaminated with any household cleaners, detergents, or any other substance that might potentially be toxic to marine organisms. It's also a good idea to mark your buckets as "clean salt water only" or "wastewater only" with an indelible marker, so you never have to worry about someone accidentally using them as mop buckets. If you can't find any suitable or large enough buckets at your local hardware store, ask the manager of a fast-food restaurant if he'll sell you some empty five-gallon pickle buckets. Bakeries are also a good source, since they usually get many of their frostings and other ingredients in large food-grade buckets as well. In many cases, these buckets would just be bound for the garbage dumpster anyway, and the manager might be happy to part with them at a reasonable price.

That being said, let's get back to mixing our salt water. At this stage, you'll need a high-quality synthetic salt mix, a hydrometer (either the swing-needle variety or a standard floating one), a plastic or wooden stirring stick, and RO purified tap water. Begin adding water either directly to the tank or to a separate bucket. The tank should be filled no more than ¾ of the way. The remaining 25 percent of tank volume can be used to make any minor specific gravity adjustments as needed. You can fill the bucket as high as you like, as long as you can lift it over the aquarium without losing control and spilling some of the water or, worse yet, dropping the entire bucket onto the tank.

Slowly start stirring in the salt mix, pouring very gradually and making sure that each batch dissolves completely before adding more. If you add the salt too quickly, it won't dissolve properly, and you'll tend to get inaccurate hydrometer

readings. It's a good idea to measure out approximately one cup at a time with a plastic measuring cup so you'll have at least a vague idea of how much salt must be mixed with each gallon of water in order to reach the desired salinity level. You should also test the water with your hydrometer after each addition of salt so you'll know when the correct salinity has been reached.

Specific gravity and the role of the hydrometer

I just mentioned that you should test the salinity of your water with a hydrometer as you mix it, but this isn't entirely accurate. A hydrometer measures specific gravity, not salinity. So what's the difference? The salinity is a measure of the total amount of dissolved salts in a saltwater mixture, which is read in grams per liter, or parts per thousand. Specific gravity is an indirect measure of salinity. A hydrometer actually compares the weight of a sample of salt water with the weight of an equal volume of distilled water. The more dissolved salts that are present in the sample, the higher the specific gravity and, for all intents and purposes, the higher the salinity. For example, a water sample that has a specific gravity of 1.020 at 77 degrees Fahrenheit (25 degrees Celsius) has a salinity of 29.8 gm/liter, while a sample with a specific gravity of 1.024 at that same temperature has a salinity of 35.5 gm/liter. The two scales may measure something completely different, but there is a direct correlation between the results.

Both the swing-needle hydrometer and the traditional floating hydrometer will give accurate measurements of specific gravity, but I would recommend that you stick with the swing-needle style. I've tried both, and I find that the swing-needle models are simpler to use and much

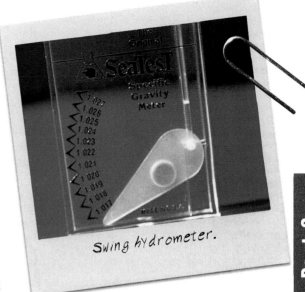

Swing hydrometer.

Handle me with care!

The common names chosen for marine fish are often based on a particular fish's color pattern, body shape, or some natural behavior it is known to exhibit. When it comes to the various members of the Acanthuridae family—the surgeon-fish—the common name should be taken as a warning to aquarists to "handle with care." All of the members of this family, though relatively peaceful in the aquarium, are equipped with scalpel-like, retractable spines on the caudal peduncle (the base of the caudal fin). These spines are capable of inflicting nasty lacerations on the fingers and hands of careless aquarists, so care must be taken when netting these fish and during routine aquarium maintenance to avoid injury.

easier to read. After all, it's hard to mistake the reading when there's a big needle pointing directly to it. With floating hydrometers, on the other hand, you have to squint your eyes to see which graduated mark on the float lines up exactly with the surface of the water in the beaker.

What is the correct specific gravity?

As I've mentioned time and time again, the water parameters in the world's oceans, especially around tropical coral reefs, are remarkably stable, and this applies equally to the specific gravity. That's not to suggest that a hydrometer reading taken in the Caribbean would be perfectly identical to one taken in the tropical Pacific or one taken from the Red Sea. Indeed, you might get radically different results from each location (up to 1.035 in the Red Sea!). On the other hand, if you were to take several measurements over the course of many years in the same location, you would get nearly identical results each time. So what does this tell us about the correct specific gravity for a marine aquarium?

As with all the other conditions, it's not the exact value of the specific gravity that counts; it's the stability. Any specific gravity measurement within the range of 1.020 and 1.024 is generally considered acceptable for most marine organisms, provided it is maintained with little or no fluctuation. Even a one-point variation, say from 1.021 to 1.022, within the course of 24 hours would be excessive and could adversely affect the health of your fish or invertebrates. To prevent such dramatic swings, it's very important to top off any fresh water lost to evaporation on a daily basis and to make sure the clean salt water you add after a partial water change has the same specific gravity as the rest of the water in the aquarium.

Why is the specific gravity in my dealer's tanks so low?

I mentioned that the ideal range for the specific gravity in a marine aquarium is between 1.020 and 1.024. Why, then, do so many dealers keep the S.G. of their aquarium water much lower than this (My dealer keeps his around 1.018)? The reason is, they're trying to minimize the number of parasites and pathogenic microorganisms that are present on the fish. Wild-caught fish, along with the various pests that are found on their bodies, are accustomed to the relatively high S.G. of the ocean. While the fish can adjust to a considerably lower S.G. (provided the transition takes place very gradually), many of the pathogenic organisms cannot, and they are subsequently killed by the osmotic shock.

What's wrong with using natural sea water?

Readers who live on or near the coast may be asking themselves, "Why go through all the trouble of purifying tap water, measuring and mixing synthetic sea salt, and testing the specific gravity over and over, when all I have to do is make a quick trip to the beach to collect a few buckets of natural sea water?" The truth of the matter is, using natural sea water in the aquarium is fraught with problems. For one thing, you wouldn't have much choice but to collect it from very close to shore, which means you'd likely be getting water contaminated with pollutants introduced through boat traffic, the dumping of raw sewage, agricultural runoff, and a host of other sources. Also, natural sea water can introduce a wide range of parasites and pathogenic microorganisms into the aquarium, some of which may be extremely difficult to eradicate once they get established. And truth be told, lugging heavy buckets full of water from the shore to your car and then transporting them home without any major spills is a logistical nightmare. You're better off mixing your own salt water, using RO purified tap water and a high-quality synthetic salt mix. That way, you can be sure that you're starting off on the right foot.

"Tweaking" the specific gravity

Let's assume that you've decided to mix the salt water for your marine aquarium in the tank itself. You've filled it three-quarters of the way with water, and you've gradually been adding synthetic salt mix one cup at a time, aiming for a target specific gravity of, say, 1.021. What happens if your last hydrometer reading indicates that the specific gravity is actually 1.022? Do you drain all of the water and start all over again? Not at all! This is exactly what you should use that remaining 25 percent of aquarium volume for. Consider it your margin of error. All you have to do is gradually dilute the water in the aquarium with a little fresh water (dechlorinated and RO-purified, of course) until the specific gravity comes down to the desired level. On the other hand, if your hydrometer reading is too low, simply continue to add salt until the specific gravity reading is high enough.

Behind the scenes—support for live rock creates a natural, reef-like effect.

Part 2

Part 2

Adding live rock and live sand

As I've already indicated, live rock and live sand should be installed only after the aquarium has been partially filled with water. To ensure that the beneficial encrusting and sand-sifting organisms are not exposed to wildly fluctuating salinity levels, it's highly recommended that you mix your salt water to the correct specific gravity in a separate container, rather than in the aquarium itself, if you intend to use live rock or live sand. As a general rule, you'll want to use 1 to 1½ pounds of live rock per gallon of water. This amount of rock can displace a considerable amount of water, so the tank should be no more than half full when you add the rock. Be sure to have extra salt water mixed and ready in the likely event that you'll still need to top off the aquarium after adding the rock.

When positioning the live rock on top of its base-rock foundation, keep in mind that every live rock technically has an upside and a downside. In other words, the side of the rock that was exposed as it lay on the ocean floor should be facing upward in the aquarium as well. Why? That portion of the rock likely will be more heavily encrusted with organisms requiring oxygenated conditions and at least some exposure to sunlight. The side of the rock that was in contact with the ocean floor (perhaps even partially buried in the sand), on the other hand, should face downward in the aquarium. Reverse this position, and you risk losing most of the desirable encrusting organisms, the whole reason you paid the long dollar for live rock in the first place.

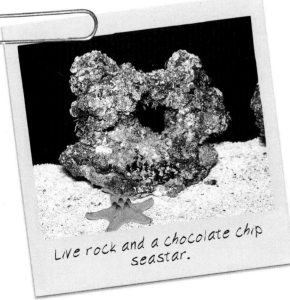

Live rock and a chocolate chip seastar.

When adding live sand, it's very easy to cloud the aquarium with tiny white particles. This can be avoided, or at least minimized, by very slowly lowering the plastic bag containing the sand until it comes to rest on the bottom of the aquarium. Pinch the top of the bag closed with your fingers so none of the sand can escape as you lower it. Once you have it resting on the bottom, gently tip it over, and pour out the contents. The slower you pour, the less water clouding you'll experience. Then, very gently and evenly spread the sand across the bottom of the tank with your hands.

Once the live rock and/or sand are in place, and the aquarium is filled to capacity with salt water of the correct specific gravity, the protein skimmer should be turned on immediately to remove any dissolved pollutants introduced with the rock or sand. No matter how diligently you may have cleaned and cured the rock ahead of time, it's still very likely that some die-off will continue to occur within the aquarium, and the skimmer will help to minimize the impact to your water quality.

Live sand and live rock.

Making sure all systems are "go"

Okay, your rockwork, substrate, and decorations are in place, your protein skimmer is skimming along nicely, and your aquarium is finally filled with salt water. It's time to "fire up" the rest of the equipment to make sure everything is working as it should be. But before plugging anything in, carefully examine all of the equipment power cords to make sure none is damaged or frayed. Try to rout the cords in a neat, organized fashion, so they are easily accessible but still hidden from view as much as possible. Also, make sure there is a bend or loop in the middle of each power cord so salt water cannot travel straight down the cord into the power outlet, causing a short. If your light fixture is suspended over the aquarium, make sure it is high enough so that water cannot splash onto it easily, or place a tight-fitting cover glass over the aquarium.

If you haven't done so already, consider using a ground-fault-circuit interrupter (GFI) in conjunction with all of the electrical equipment. A GFI will instantaneously disrupt the flow of current to an electrical device in the event of accidental immersion. I was extremely grateful to have this technology several years back when I accidentally dropped a fluorescent hood into a 29-gallon freshwater aquarium, lit of course. Knowing full well that electricity and water are a lethal combination, I tried to grab the fixture as it fell into the water out of reflex. The hood was a total loss, but I, luckily, escaped unscathed thanks to the GFI.

Once you've taken all necessary steps to minimize the danger of electrocution, it's safe to plug in your heater, lights, and filtration equipment. Give everything a thorough "once

Part 2

Why don't anemones sting clownfish?

Nearly everyone has heard of the symbiotic relationship between clownfish and their anemone hosts. But how is it possible for a clownfish to nestle peacefully among the tentacles of an anemone without being stung to death? The answer lies in the special protective mucus coating secreted by the clownfish. Not only can this mucus neutralize the toxins delivered by the anemone's stinging cells, but it also effectively masks the clownfish's chemical signature so that the anemone does not identify it as either a prey item or a potential predator.

Some research suggests that a clownfish's "immunity" to an anemone's sting is not automatic. Rather, when introduced to a new anemone, a clownfish must make several tentative passes through the anemone's tentacles to pick up specific proteins from the anemone and incorporate them into its mucus coating. Once this has been achieved, the clownfish can safely retreat into the anemone. However, if the clownfish is frightened into the anemone before the process is completed, it can be stung to death.

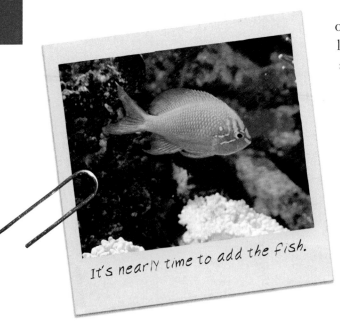

It's nearly time to add the fish.

over" to make sure there are no malfunctions, excessively loud motors, leaky connections, and so on. If you're using a wet-dry biofilter, you might need to adjust the height of the intake chamber up or down slightly at this point in order to keep the water level in both the aquarium and sump in equilibrium. When you're satisfied that everything is operating as it should, you can leave all the equipment up and running as if the fish or invertebrates are already in the aquarium. Before too long, you'll be ready to introduce your first specimens, but there's one major hurdle yet to be overcome, the cycling process.

Hurry Up and Wait: Cycling the Aquarium

It's at this stage of the aquarium set-up process that many budding aquarists begin to lose patience and choose to rush headlong into the introduction of animals. After all, why wait? All of the equipment is fully functional, the temperature and specific gravity are right on target, and the water looks crystal clear. What better time to add the fish or invertebrates? Actually, this is the worst time to introduce them. In fact, to do so now would likely result in the death of all the desired creatures in the tank and, subsequently, despair and loss of interest on the part of the aquarist.

"New tank syndrome"

Unfortunately, this sudden, seemingly unexplainable loss of newly introduced specimens–known in the

Damsels, like this *Chrysiptera cyanea*, are often used to cycle the tank.

Part 2

Is conspicuous coloration a drawback?

It somehow seems counterproductive for so many reef fish to be brilliantly colored. With hordes of hungry predators about, one would think that brightly colored fish would be easily preyed upon. But surprisingly, brilliant coloration is not necessarily a handicap on the coral reef. For one thing, brighter colors can help fish identify other individuals of the same species for spawning purposes—a major plus when you consider the vast number of fish that live on and around the coral reef. Also, many of the sessile invertebrates inhabiting the reef are fairly brightly colored themselves, so the fish don't necessarily stand out against the backdrop of the coral reef.

As far as predators are concerned, most of them emerge at dusk to feed, and in the twilight, all those brightly colored fish become, for all intents and purposes, invisible. Besides, the red-yellow portions of the visible light spectrum can only penetrate a few feet into salt water, so fish sporting those particular colors will tend to look grayer at depth, even when the sun is at the highest point in the sky.

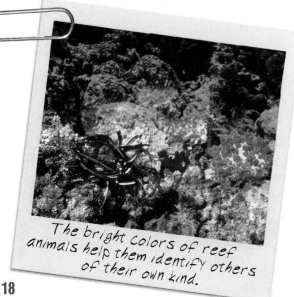

The bright colors of reef animals help them identify others of their own kind.

hobby as "new tank syndrome" (NTS)—occurs more often than it should among novice freshwater and marine aquarists. It's also a huge "confidence buster" for newcomers, many of whom simply abandon the hobby in frustration after all of their efforts and expenditures come to naught.

But the good news is, NTS is completely avoidable. All you have to do is give your new marine aquarium adequate time to "cycle" before introducing any valuable specimens. If you're making the transition to salt water from fresh water, you're probably already familiar with the concept of cycling, and the process is, for all intents and purposes, identical. For those unfamiliar with the concept, cycling simply means allowing the beneficial nitrifying bacteria–the same ones we examined in the chapter on biological filtration–to become fully established within the aquarium. Remember, without ample colonies of nitrobacters to convert ammonia to less harmful compounds, any specimens that you place in your aquarium are at risk of literally being poisoned by their own waste.

Is cycling a catch-22?

Right now you might be asking yourself, "If nitrifying bacteria use fish waste as a fuel source, how can I get them to proliferate without first introducing some fish? Isn't that a catch-22?" Indeed, it would be if fish waste were the only source of ammonia, which, fortunately, it is not. You can jumpstart the cycling process just as easily by adding a pinch of flake food or a little liquid invertebrate food to the water each day. As the food decomposes, it will produce the necessary ammonia to initiate the cycle. Another tried-and-true method is to add ammonium chloride, an inorganic source of ammonia that can be purchased at any chemical supply store, to the aquarium at a rate of approximately 1.5 milliliters per 8 gallons of water. The bacteria don't care what the source is, whether organic or inorganic, as long as they have ammonia as a fuel to get the cycle going.

Damsels as guinea pigs

It was once common practice among marine aquarists (and probably still is for some) to introduce one or two inexpensive, hardy fish–usually damsels–to initiate the cycling process. The poor creatures would be forced to endure spiking ammonia and nitrite levels as colonies of nitrifying bacteria became established and began to do their work. Those lucky enough to survive the ordeal might then be traded to another aquarist who would likely use them to cycle yet another aquarium, and they'd find themselves right back where they started–swimming in toxic water. If the fish survived and were left to inhabit the newly cycled aquarium, a different problem would often arise; the highly territorial damsels would claim the entire tank for themselves, making the introduction of additional specimens extremely problematic. While there's no question that the "damsel method" was (is?) a fairly reliable way to cycle a new marine aquarium, one could certainly make the argument that using fish as "guinea pigs" or, more accurately, "canaries in the coal mine" is not the most ethical approach to cycling–no matter how expendable we may think they are.

Hand-me-down colonies

Another way to help the cycling process along is to "borrow" some existing colonies of nitrifying bacteria from an established aquarium. This can be done by taking

Live sand is a great source of starter bacteria.

Damselfish like this Chromis viridis are ideal starter fish.

Part 2

a filter medium (sponge, spun-nylon floss, etc.) or a scoop of substrate from the "mature" aquarium and placing it in your new system. As long as you also provide oxygenated conditions, ample surface area, and a source of ammonia, this hand-me-down colony will quickly spread throughout the rest of the aquarium. Of course, high-quality (extremely porous) live rock is also an excellent source of beneficial nitrifying bacteria, and the more pieces you add, the more rapidly the aquarium will cycle. Just be sure to clean and cure the live rock as previously described, or you may end up overwhelming the system with pollutants produced by decomposing organisms.

Consider the source!

It's very important to consider the source when borrowing gravel or a filter medium from an existing tank in order to inoculate a new system. Under no circumstances should you accept such materials from an aquarium that has recently contained a sick or dying animal, especially if you intend to use it to cycle a mini-reef. It's not that you need to worry so much about introducing parasites or pathogenic microorganisms into your new system. Few if any of these organisms will survive the entire cycling period, which can take up to a month or more, without a host organism being present (i.e., a fish or invertebrate to infect). A more serious concern is that you may inadvertently release traces of medication into your new aquarium, some of which can be harmful to some fish and invertebrates and very difficult to eliminate completely from the system.

Over-the-counter colonies

Yet another way to kick the cycling process into high gear is to use one of the numerous liquid or dry-media cycling products, which can be purchased by mail order or from your local aquarium dealer. These products contain live cultures of beneficial nitrifying bacteria, which can easily be added to the aquarium water to supplement the existing microbial population. However, it's important to keep in mind that you can't just dump one of these products into the aquarium on the first day after filling it with salt water and assume the cycling process is complete. Without oxygenated conditions and a sufficiently high level of ammonia to sustain them, the bacteria would simply die off, and you'd be back to square one.

To test or not to test, that is the question!

So, we've established that cycling an aquarium can take as long as a month or more, but isn't there some way to determine the exact number of days or weeks we must wait for cycling to occur? If all things were equal from one aquarium to the next, perhaps we could establish some precise time frame, but such is not the case. Even subtle differences in the filtration media used, the type of substrate and rockwork, the amount of turbulence that is created at the surface of the aquarium, and the amount of nitrogenous "food" that is introduced into the water can have a significant impact on the rate of the cycling process. Simply put, the better job you do of providing the three essential elements that nitrifying bacteria need for survival, the faster the cycling process will go.

While we cannot predict exactly how long it will take to cycle a given aquarium, we can certainly monitor the process by testing the water regularly with ammonia, nitrite, and nitrate test kits. These relatively inexpensive kits are available at any aquarium shop, and they are remarkably easy to use–even for us non-scientific types. Though the instructions will vary slightly from test kit to test kit, typically all you have to do is fill a small vial with aquarium water, add a predetermined amount of the test chemical–either in tablet or liquid form–to the water, shake the vial, and wait a few minutes for the water to change color. Then, you simply compare the color of the water to the color chart included with the kit (preferably against a white background). Each color on the comparator chart will match a specific level of ammonia, nitrite, or nitrate, depending on what you're testing for, which will be indicated in parts per million (ppm) or milligrams per liter (mg/l).

During the first several days of the cycling process, you should get very high readings of

Jumpstart Your Cycle (Without using damsels)

There are several methods you can employ to kick your nitrifying bacteria into high gear, without subjecting damsels to cruel and unusual treatment. Possibilities include:

• Adding a pinch of flake food or a few drops of liquid invertebrate food to your aquarium's water each day

• Adding ammonium chloride (an inorganic source of ammonia) to the water at a rate of 1.5 milliliters per 8 gallons of water

• "Borrowing" a colony of nitrifying bacteria (a filter medium or a scoop of substrate from an established aquarium)

• Using a commercial cycling product in conjunction with one of the aforementioned ammonia sources.

Part 2

Test the water until all results are within normal range.

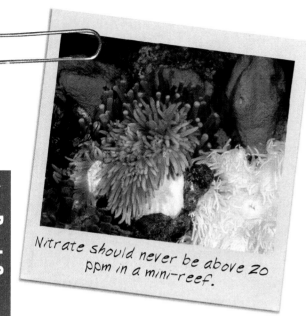

Nitrate should never be above 20 ppm in a mini-reef.

Part 2

ammonia. As colonies of nitrobacters begin to flourish in response to the elevated ammonia level, testing will eventually indicate a precipitous drop in the ammonia level and a spike in the nitrite level. The nitrite level will continue to rise until the nitrifying bacteria begin to proliferate. At that point, the nitrite level will drop and the nitrate level will begin to climb. The aquarium is considered fully cycled once testing indicates no measurable ammonia or nitrite. A large water change–at least 50 percent, though some would suggest changing as much as 100 percent of the water–should be performed at this stage to dilute the nitrate. Fish can generally tolerate nitrate levels up to approximately 40ppm. However, for the mini-reef, nitrate should never be allowed to accumulate beyond 20ppm. Some of the more delicate sessile invertebrates will even suffer at that concentration, so the best bet for reefkeepers is to maintain the nitrate level as close to zero as possible.

But what if you don't want to fool around with all those vials and chemicals? Is it safe to cycle the aquarium without monitoring the ammonia, nitrite, and nitrate levels with test kits? The answer is a very tentative "yes." Technically, if you were to keep the aquarium running for four or five weeks while adding a nitrogenous food source each day, you could probably perform a major water change at the end of the fifth week and start introducing specimens.

Tips for ensuring accurate test results

- Always use test kits from the same manufacturer and product line. There is some variability in accuracy between different manufacturers' products.

- Avoid using out-dated test kits. The chemical reagents are only viable for a certain amount of time. A use-by date should be listed on the product's packaging.

- Follow the manufacturer's instructions to the letter.

- Always test at the same time of day. Some water parameters will vary slightly depending on the time of day.

- Store your test kits out of direct sunlight in a cool, dry location to increase their longevity.

- Keep a record of your test results in a log or journal so you can monitor any changes that take place over a long period of time.

The only trouble is, words like "probably" and "technically" aren't very reassuring when it comes to keeping very costly and most likely wild-collected marine specimens alive in captivity. You and your specimens will be much better off if you monitor the cycling process carefully with test kits. That way, you can be certain when it's safe to introduce them to the aquarium.

A very delicate balance

Once cycling is complete, it's safe to begin adding livestock to your new marine aquarium. This should be accomplished very gradually. Add no more than two or three fish or invertebrates at first, and give them a few weeks to get adjusted to their new surroundings before adding more specimens. If you

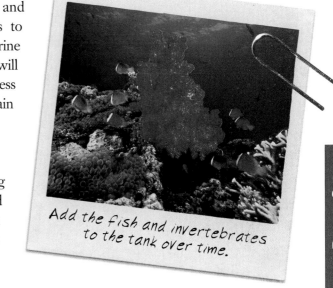

Add the fish and invertebrates to the tank over time.

introduce too many organisms too quickly, the bacteria that make up your biological filter will not be able to keep pace with the excessive "bioload," and you may experience a sudden ammonia spike. On the other hand, if you introduce additional specimens every few weeks, while continuing to test for ammonia and nitrite, you won't upset the delicate balance that exists between the biofilter and the bioload, and your new fish and/or invertebrates will have a much better chance of surviving the transition. This is very important not only from the standpoint of conservation, but also because early success in the saltwater hobby can make the difference between sticking with it for a lifetime and quitting prematurely out of frustration.

Another factor that can upset the delicate balance of the biological filter is the amount of food that you provide for your new charges. Overfeeding is a very common mistake among novice and experienced aquarists alike. It's just so hard to resist dropping in another pinch of flake food or another helping of frozen brine shrimp when the fish keep giving you those "puppy dog" eyes that seem to say, "I know you just fed me an hour ago, but I'm feeling faint with hunger." The problem is, most fish will give you that look every time you pass the tank (after all, they know on which side their bread is buttered!), and consistently giving in to their begging will not only overwhelm the biofilter, but it will also lead to significant health problems for your fish further down the road.

Important Water Parameters

Thus far, we've discussed the importance of stability in the marine environment as it applies to temperature, specific gravity, and various aspects of water-quality management. In this chapter, we'll take a closer look at certain characteristics of salt water and the specific water parameters you'll need to maintain with a high degree of stability in order to achieve success with your new marine aquarium. We'll also discuss some of the important supplements and trace elements that you'll need to be familiar with if you intend to keep a mini-reef.

At the risk of sounding redundant (although it may be too late for that already!), the water parameters in the world's oceans, especially in the areas around coral reefs, are remarkably stable in quality and

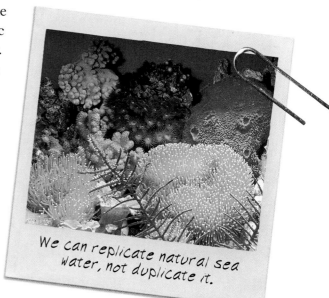

We can replicate natural sea water, not duplicate it.

chemical composition (that is, if you discount the presence of the various pollutants introduced through human activities). Our main responsibility as aquarists is to replicate the conditions that marine fish and invertebrates have adapted to in their natural environment as closely as possible and to take all necessary steps to prevent them from fluctuating to a significant degree.

Electronic pH meters make short work of pH testing.

pH and carbonate hardness

One of the more important parameters you'll need to become familiar with and monitor carefully is the pH of your aquarium's water. Readers who have a background in chemistry will bristle at this definition, but to keep things simple, pH is a measure of how acidic or alkaline the water is. Any pH measurement below 7.0 (neutral) is considered to be more acidic, while measurements above 7.0 are considered more alkaline. Technically, alkalinity is a measure of the carbonate hardness, or buffering capacity, of the water. In simple terms, buffering capacity can be defined as the water's ability to resist a change in pH. In most cases, when a drop in pH occurs, the problem can be rectified through the addition of buffering compounds. Fortunately, buffering compounds are normally included in most high-quality synthetic sea salt mixes, so each time you perform a partial water change, these compounds are re-introduced. Frequent small water changes, using a quality salt mix, will go a long way toward maintaining the water's alkalinity, and therefore its pH, at the desired level.

So, what is the desired level? The pH of natural sea water ranges between 8.2 and 8.4, which is relatively high compared to fresh water. One notable exception is the fresh water found in Africa's rift lakes (Tanganyika, Malawi, etc.), which has a pH value very similar to that of sea water. The exact value of the pH in your new marine aquarium is not as important as the stability of the pH, as long as it remains within the desired range with little or no fluctuation.

Factors influencing pH

As I've already mentioned, most high-quality synthetic salt mixes contain buffering compounds that will keep the pH of your water properly elevated. However, several factors can cause pH to drop in spite of the presence of these buffers. For example, the waste materials and the byproducts of the metabolic processes of various marine organisms tend to be highly acidic and will gradually lower pH over time if allowed to accumulate. Decomposing food items and the acidic compounds produced during the nitrification cycle will also contribute to this pH-lowering trend. It stands to reason, then, that "crashing" pH levels can be a major problem in an aquarium that is overstocked and overfed. So what can you do to counteract this trend? Obviously, the most important thing you can do is to avoid overstocking and overfeeding, but the next best things is to stay on top of those routine partial water changes! The more often you change the water, the less pronounced the swings in pH will be, even if you tend to overfeed on occasion or you sometimes fall victim to "one more pretty fish syndrome."

No deadbeat dads here!

Can you guess the name of the fish that has a tail like a monkey, a pouch like a kangaroo, and the head of a horse? If you answered "the seahorse," you guessed right! Seahorses (*Hippocampus* spp.) are indeed an odd assemblage of "spare parts" taken from various members of the animal kingdom. In fact, their appearance is so strange (albeit irresistible) that many people are unaware that they're actually fish. But their strangeness doesn't end with their appearance. In the world of the seahorse, it is the male that becomes pregnant and incubates the young. The female deposits her eggs into a specialized pouch on the male's belly, where the male fertilizes them. The male then protects and tends to the eggs until they are ready to hatch.

Other factors affecting pH are completely natural and have nothing to do with neglect or poor husbandry on the part of the aquarist. For instance, certain invertebrates utilize the same elements that buffer pH to build their calcareous shells and skeletons, which effectively reduces the buffering capacity of the water and, hence, lowers the pH. Also, various marine algae, whether cultivated or unintentionally introduced, can contribute to pH fluctuations through their natural photosynthetic activity. Like all plants, algae utilize carbon dioxide and produce oxygen during the day. However, when night falls and the lights are no longer on to promote photosynthesis, the process is reversed, and the algae begin to produce carbon dioxide instead of oxygen. Since carbon dioxide is acidic, the pH in the aquarium will tend to drop slightly whenever the lights are turned off.

Again, water changes are the key to overcoming these problems. Frequent water changes will not only help to replenish the buffering agents that are routinely used up for shell and skeleton production by certain invertebrates, but they will also keep the dissolved nutrient level in the aquarium low, thereby minimizing the proliferation of unwanted algae and discouraging the production of pH-lowering carbon dioxide at night.

Testing for pH

Of course, in order to stay on top of any changes in pH, you'll need to test your aquarium's water routinely with a test kit. Be sure to buy a kit formulated specifically for testing salt water rather than fresh water as the two are not interchangeable. Freshwater pH test kits generally measure from 6.0 up to 7.6, while most saltwater kits measure from 7.6 to 8.4. Testing for pH, which should be performed on a weekly basis, is done in exactly the same fashion as are the tests for ammonia, nitrite, and nitrate. You simply fill the vial with aquarium water, add a few drops of the test chemical liquid, shake the vial, and compare the color of the water to the color comparator chart included with the kit. As I mentioned previously, any stable reading within the range of 8.2 to 8.4 is acceptable. If the pH should fall below that range, you'll need to determine the cause of the problem and make the necessary correction immediately. This may mean cutting back on the amount you're feeding, reducing the number of specimens in the tank, or locating and removing a dead animal from somewhere in the aquarium system.

Should you use supplements?

Certain elements and minerals that occur naturally in sea water, such as calcium, iodine, strontium, and several other trace elements, are drawn from the water and utilized by various marine organisms for a wide range of biological processes. It stands to reason, then, that these same elements in nearly the same concentrations should be provided for the fish or invertebrates in the marine aquarium in order to keep them in optimum health. The only difference is, in the closed system of the aquarium, the organisms gradually deplete these elements, but there is no natural means of replacing them. The processes of protein skimming and chemical filtration with activated carbon also remove them from the water. So, how do you go about putting these vital elements back into the aquarium system once they're all used up?

In the fish-only aquarium, these elements are replaced in sufficient amounts whenever a partial water change is performed, provided a high-quality synthetic salt mix is used. However, in the mini-reef, the invertebrates tend to extract some of these elements from the water so rapidly that partial water changes cannot keep pace, and it may become necessary to replenish them with supplements.

Calcium

Calcium is, perhaps, the element of greatest concern for both reef aquarists and fish-only aquarists as it is required for the health of all marine organisms. It is especially important for organisms that produce skeletons, exoskeletons, or shells out of calcium carbonate, including certain corals, crustaceans, tubeworms, mollusks, and echinoderms, in other words, most of the organisms of interest to the reef aquarist. Fish also use calcium to promote skeletal growth.

The desired calcium level for the marine aquarium is approximately 400 mg/liter (roughly 400 parts per million), which can be monitored routinely and easily with a calcium hardness test kit available at any aquarium shop. Whenever testing indicates that the calcium concentration is beginning to dip below the desired level, you can bring it back up by adding a commercial liquid calcium supplement to the aquarium.

Do-it-yourself calcium supplement

If you enjoy tinkering with chemicals, you can also produce your own calcium additive, which is known in the hobby as kalkwasser or limewater. This is done by mixing calcium hydroxide powder with RO-purified water in a durable container until no more powder can be dissolved. Cap the container, and allow the solution to stand for 24 hours. A certain percentage of the powder will settle to the bottom of the container. This powder should not be added to the aquarium. Only the clear liquid should be decanted and used in the aquarium. You can, however, use the powder that settles out of solution to produce additional batches of limewater as needed.

If you decide to make your own limewater, you must be extremely cautious during the entire process. Both the calcium hydroxide powder and the limewater solution are highly caustic, and the chemical reaction produces considerable heat. Goggles, gloves, and a dust mask are highly recommended attire whenever making the solution or handling the powder. Also, limewater is extremely alkaline (with a pH around 12!) and must be added to the water very gradually to avoid raising the pH beyond the desired range. Considering the dangers involved, and the hit-or-miss nature of supplementing calcium with homemade limewater, you may be more comfortable using an off-the-shelf calcium additive. It may end

Part 2

Kalkwasser recipe

You'll need:

- 3 level teaspoons of calcium hydroxide powder
- 1 gallon of RO-purified water
- 1 pair of rubber gloves
- 1 dust mask

(Protective goggles or eyeglasses)

Don the dust mask, rubber gloves, and protective goggles. Add the calcium hydroxide to the RO-purified water. Stir very gently to prevent carbon dioxide from entering the mixture and creating calcium carbonate. Continue stirring until the water has absorbed as much of the powder as possible. Any powder that can't be absorbed will settle to the bottom of the container. Cap the container, and let it settle for a few hours. Decant the clear liquid, in very small doses, into the aquarium until the desired calcium level is reached.

Some common marine algae.

up costing you a little more, but the added certainty and peace-of-mind is worth a few extra pennies.

Iodine and strontium

Two elements that are also vital to the health and well being of marine organisms are iodine and strontium. Iodine is especially critical if you intend to cultivate certain marine macroalgae, such as the various species of *Caulerpa* and *Halimeda*, which are very popular among reef aquarists. The desired levels are 60 micrograms per liter for iodine and 7.9 mg/liter for strontium. Both can be supplemented with easy-to-use liquid additives, but neither can be monitored with a commercially manufactured test kit. This means that it is very important to adhere strictly to the manufacturer's recommendations when determining the rate and frequency of supplementation.

There are several additional trace elements found in sea water that are vital to the metabolic processes of various marine organisms (In fact, all of the elements known to science are present in small amounts in sea water), and most are available in the form of liquid supplements, either singly or combined with other elements. However, since there is much yet to be learned about how individual trace elements affect the health of different marine organisms (not to mention the fact that many trace elements do not have corresponding test kits), it's very important to use them judiciously. Some experts even recommend using supplements at half the recommended strength at first to see how the invertebrates in the mini-reef respond. If all goes well, you can gradually increase the dose to three-quarters of the recommended rate and then to the full rate. Perhaps the most important thing to remember about using trace element supplements is that even the best additives on the market won't compensate for poor maintenance practices or a lack of timely water changes.

Grape Caulerpa,
Caulerpa racemosa.

Part Three
Getting Stocked

"Mr. Peterson, I'm sorry that you can't help eating everything your owner puts in your tank, but you just have to learn some self-control."

The Payoff!

You've finally made it through the tedious set-up and cycling phases; all of your filtration, heating, and lighting systems are up and running, and testing indicates that your water parameters are well within the ideal range. Now it's time for your patience to start paying off! It's time to add some animals to your new marine aquarium! Selecting organisms is, far and away, the most fun and satisfying stage of putting together a marine aquarium. There are so many delightful fish and invertebrates to choose from that it can seem almost impossible to narrow down your options to just a handful of specimens.

However, it's critical to proceed with caution when deciding which specimens to include in your

This tall tank is sensibly stocked with a just a few fish.

Handle with Care!
Lionfish can hurt!

Dascyllus trimaculatus, the
two-spot, or domino damsel.

aquarium. The stocking decisions you make at this stage will determine whether you will ultimately experience a beautiful assortment of peaceful and compatible species or a tank full of mismatched organisms that are constantly squabbling at the slightest provocation. The key to achieving the former and avoiding the latter is to do a little advance research. But where to begin?

Research sources

Your best bet is to head for the library or bookstore to check out or buy a few additional marine aquarium reference books. I've tried to include all of the vital information about livestock selection within the pages of this book, but it's always helpful to read what other authors have to say on the subject as well. There are many excellent books out there that are well suited for beginners interested in learning about the characteristics and requirements of different marine species. Aquarium magazines and journals are also excellent sources of information on species selection. If you haven't done so already, you might consider getting a regular subscription to one of these publications. Of course, if you have access to the Internet, you can also gather lots of useful information about fish and invertebrates on line. Just keep in mind that there is no editor looking over Internet materials to verify accuracy. In other words, a lot of wacky information and spectacular claims can make their way onto the Net, so you have to be wary of your sources.

Learning from fellow aquarists

Another way to learn about different marine organisms is to consult with other fish enthusiasts or invert aficionados who may have hands-on

Everything I need to know I learned from T.F.H.

If you subscribe to *Tropical Fish Hobbyist* magazine make a point of hanging on to your old copies. I've been a loyal *TFH* subscriber for almost a decade, and I've kept every single issue. Believe me, they come in handy. Whenever I come across an unfamiliar fish or invertebrate that I feel compelled to keep, I can almost always find the animal's care requirements, or at least some tidbit of information about a closely related species, somewhere in my backlog of copies. In the past, I've even used various articles as "blueprints" for setting up a particular species tank or to help me choose compatible species for a marine community. I guess you could say that I learned everything I need to know about marine aquariums from the pages of *TFH*.

experience in keeping some of the species that interest you. You can connect with fellow marine aquarists through your local aquarium society or, perhaps, through Internet chat rooms. Your dealer might even be able to help you get in touch with other marine aquarists in your area who might be willing to share the benefit of their experience. Who knows, you might have a tremendous source of information living right next door to you!

Finding a reputable dealer

The surest way to end up with a peaceful and compatible community of marine organisms is to solicit the advice of an experienced, reputable dealer. Look for someone who is willing to spend a little time–even when business is hopping on a Saturday afternoon–to help you find the right fish or invertebrates for your needs and who is capable of giving thoughtful and thorough answers to any questions you might have about the organisms offered for sale. You can also tell a lot about a dealer by the condition of his aquariums. If every other tank has a dead fish floating in it, or the water in the tanks is the color and consistency of pea soup, it's probably a wise idea to shop elsewhere. On the other hand, you can safely assume that a dealer who devotes lots of time and attention to aquarium maintenance will be equally inclined to lavish attention on customers.

More often than not, the right dealer will be the sole proprietor of a small aquarium shop who has had many years of personal experience in keeping both fish and invertebrates. I'm not suggesting that the

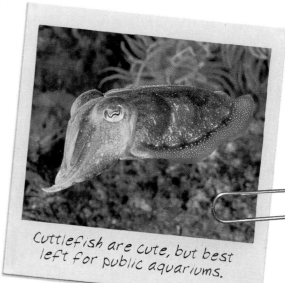

Cuttlefish are cute, but best left for public aquariums.

The long nose of Forcipiger longirostris gives a clue to special feeding needs.

young sales clerk with all the tattoos and body piercings at "Sam's Discount Fish-O-Rama" doesn't know what he's talking about. Who knows, he may only be working there to pay the bills while he finishes his degree in Marine Biology. It's just that I've generally gotten better advice, more encouragement, and fewer "bum steers" from small-business owners over the years.

Where in the world do the fish come from?

Experience isn't the only important criterion you should look for when "shopping" for a dealer. A qualified dealer should also be able to tell you with a good degree of certainty where and how his specimens are collected. This is important because in certain parts of the world (i.e., the Philippines), reef fish are sometimes poisoned with a sodium cyanide solution to make them easier to capture. As you can imagine, fish collected in this manner seldom survive for long in the aquarium. Cyanide-poisoned fish often seem perfectly healthy at the time of purchase and may even eat heartily once introduced to their new home. However, within a matter of weeks, the cyanide damage will take its toll, and most of these fish will perish suddenly. The poor unwitting aquarist is typically left wondering what went wrong and what could have been done differently to save the fish's life.

The high cost of cyanide collection

The collection of tropical marine fish with sodium cyanide, which surprisingly is still going on in certain parts of the world, is both destructive and self-defeating for those who practice it. Not only does cyanide collection exact a heavy toll on tropical marine fish sought after by aquarists, but it also destroys scores of fish and other marine organisms that have no value to the aquarium industry but, nonetheless, are vital to the ecology of the reefs.

Even more discouraging is the toll that cyanide collection takes on the coral reef itself. When cyanide collectors squirt this noxious solution into the cracks and crevices of the reef in order to anesthetize the fish they're after, they unwittingly destroy the corals and other sessile invertebrates that comprise the reefs, hence undermining their own livelihoods. Once the corals are destroyed, the fish that live among them soon vanish, and a once-thriving habitat disappears forever.

Choose a conservation-minded dealer

A good dealer is someone who encourages conservation programs by offering captive-bred fish and aquacultured invertebrates for sale instead of just specimens collected from the wild. In most cases, specimens propagated in captivity will cost more than their wild-caught counterparts, but they are well worth the added cost. Captive-bred specimens are better adapted to aquarium conditions and more likely to adjust to a diet of standard aquarium fare, and buying them helps to reduce collection pressure on wild populations, some of which have been sorely depleted over the years as a result of questionable collection practices.

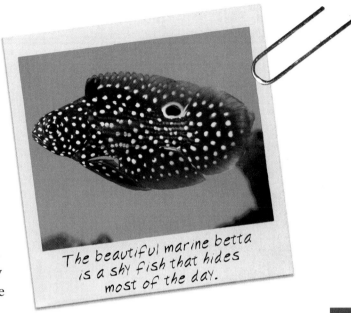

The beautiful marine betta is a shy fish that hides most of the day.

Selecting specimens for the fish-only aquarium

Once you've settled on a qualified dealer and armed yourself with information about the specific animals you'd like to keep, you're ready to purchase your first specimens. If you're stocking a fish-only aquarium, there are certain things to look for when buying fish. First, carefully examine each specimen for evidence of disease or parasitic infection, such as tiny white spots, velvety patches, cloudy eyes, ulcerations, warts or lumps, rotting fins, irregular or rapid movement, or scraping against objects in the tank. If any of these symptoms (or any other characteristics that seem out of the ordinary) are present either on the fish you'd like to purchase or on other fish in the same tank, do yourself a favor and pass the specimen by. It may be frustrating to have to postpone buying your fish after having waited so long already, but it's even more

The blue-girdled angelfish, *Pomacanthus navarchus*.

Synchiropus splendidus, the mandarin-fish, is best kept in a mini-reef aquarium.

Gramma loreto, the royal gramma, is a fine fish for beginners.

frustrating to watch costly specimens die shortly after you purchase them. And, unfortunately, most dealers do not offer guarantees on marine livestock.

It's also a good idea to make sure each fish is feeding properly before you buy. A malnourished fish will often have a pinched-in belly, as opposed to a healthy, well-rounded belly, and may sulk or remain hidden from view behind the rockwork or decorations instead of swimming actively. A conscientious dealer will make sure each fish is actively feeding before putting it out for sale, but if you're uncertain whether a fish is feeding or not, ask the dealer to feed it in front of you. Most reputable dealers will be more than happy to oblige. After all, it's in their best interest to "move" the fish in a timely manner. You can also take this opportunity to find out which particular foods are preferred by the fish you'd like to buy.

Plan your purchase, and stick to the plan!

The best approach to buying your first fish is to settle on a combination of hardy "bread-and-butter" species that you know will get along well in your aquarium and buy only those particular fish when you head for the aquarium shop. If your dealer doesn't have what you're looking for when you're ready to buy, he most likely will within a week or so. Don't be discouraged if you have to make repeated visits to your dealer to get exactly what you're after. Success is worth the wait!

Also, if at all possible, try to resist the temptation to purchase fish that you are unfamiliar with or that your dealer knows little about—no matter how beautiful they may be! Introducing a fish of uncertain deportment and dietary needs is almost always a recipe for disaster. That tiny, demure fish of uncertain origin that you just couldn't resist might eventually reach a mature size that is way beyond the carrying capacity of your

Part 3

aquarium, or it may become extremely territorial and "declare war" on every other fish in the tank. Worse yet, it may turn out to be a highly specialized feeder that won't settle for any of the standard foods you offer and ultimately wastes away before your eyes.

The compatibility question

It's not unusual for two marine fish of the same species (conspecifics) to battle to the death when confined within the same aquarium—even species that are known to congregate in massive schools in nature. Why? For one thing, even though certain fish tend to school in the wild, each individual may still stake out a small section of the reef for its own territory. In the aquarium, the available "real estate" is so greatly diminished that territorial disputes are almost inevitable between fish that naturally occupy the same ecological niche. Another reason is that a natural pecking order usually exists within wild fish populations, especially among haremic species. But if two conspecifics collected from different populations are placed in the same aquarium, fighting will likely occur until a new pecking order is established. Unfortunately, the weaker or less aggressive fish often dies—either gradually as a result of the stress from constant bickering or quickly from actual physical trauma inflicted by the stronger fish.

As a general rule, it's best to keep only one member of a species in a given aquarium community. This rule also extends to fish of different species that are very similar in coloration, body shape, and/or the ecological niche they occupy. There are, or course,

The percula clownfish is readily available wherever marine fishes are sold.

The pixy hawkfish, *Cirrhitichthys oxycephalus*.

Part 3

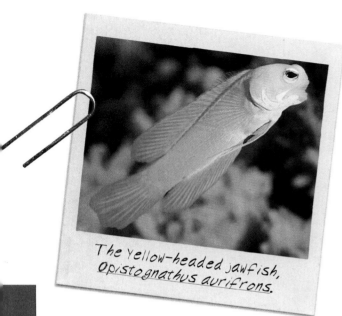

The yellow-headed jawfish,
Opistognathus aurifrons.

exceptions to this one-per-tank rule. For example, certain clownfish (*Amphiprion spp.*) usually will tolerate conspecifics, as will jawfish (*Opistognathus spp.*), firefish (*Nemateleotris spp.*), and cardinalfish (family Apogonidae) to name but a few. Of course, the emphasis here should be on the word "usually." Aggression can vary from individual to individual within a species, so there's no guarantee that members of a supposedly peaceful species won't fight among themselves. Also, the size of the aquarium can have an impact on the frequency and severity of territorial disputes. Obviously, it would be much harder for two feuding fish to stay out of each other's way in a 20-gallon aquarium than it would be in a 100-gallon aquarium.

The quarantine tank

One of the most important steps you can take to ensure that your community of marine fish remains healthy and disease-free is to isolate, or quarantine, each fish for at least

When Worlds Collide

My first real experience with species incompatibility involved introducing a pixy hawkfish (*Cirrhitichthys oxycephalus*) into a community of fish that happened to include a strawberry basslet (*Pseudochromis porphyreus*). Prior to the hawkfish's arrival, the basslet was extraordinarily well behaved with its tankmates, all of which were markedly different from the basslet in coloration and body shape. But once the hawkfish came on the scene and attempted to establish a territory among the rocks (once the sole domain of the basslet), all bets were off. The basslet embarked on a ruthless crusade of harassment and seemed bent on destroying the newcomer.

Anytime the basslet caught a glimpse of the hawkfish, no matter how fleeting, it would go on the warpath, chasing and nipping the poor fish until it was nearly driven to distraction. The one-sided war finally ended one morning with the hawkfish leaping out of the tank and meeting his dusty end on the hardwood floor. The lesson? Use caution when adding new fish to an established community. Even seemingly dissimilar species can be incompatible if they happen to occupy the same niche in the aquarium.

Part 3

a couple of weeks before introducing it to the main aquarium. This should be done with the first assortment of fish you buy after cycling the aquarium and with any specimens that are added later on. Quarantining the fish will give you a prolonged opportunity to observe them for any signs of disease that may not have been visible at the time of purchase. On the other hand, failure to isolate new introductions can lead to the aggravating loss of your entire fish community to disease.

Pseudochromis porphpyreus, hovers over the coral reef.

Often, fish carry disease-causing pathogens and parasites that do not immediately manifest themselves until a certain amount of time passes or the fish is placed under stress, such as being repeatedly netted, transported, and re-acclimated. If a disease should develop after you buy a particular specimen, it's preferable and easier to treat the fish in isolation rather than in the main aquarium. Besides, isolating the sick fish will ensure that the disease does not spread to the healthy fish in the community.

The quarantine tank does not need to be especially large or elaborate. A 10- to 15-gallon aquarium will generally suffice. You don't need any substrate, decorations, or special lighting, and a simple, inexpensive sponge filter will suffice for water purification. A heater should be included in the setup along with an airstone and air pump to oxygenate the water. You might also want to provide a few rocks or an overturned *terra-cotta* pot for a hiding place. Of course, the water temperature, pH, and specific gravity in the quarantine tank should be the same as they are in the main aquarium so the ailing fish will not be shocked by dramatically different water parameters once its health has been restored and it is ready to be returned to the main tank.

Proper stocking rate

Determining the total number of fish that can be maintained in good health in a given marine aquarium can be a tricky proposition, especially for those with no prior experience in fishkeeping. As you do your research and shop around for specimens, you might come across different rules you can use to determine the exact carrying capacity of your tank (a

Part 3

Rhinecanthus aculeatus, the Picasso triggerfish, a fiend in fins if ever there was one.

Apogon maculatus. Tiny and docile, this fellow makes a good tankmate.

fancy way of saying the total number of organisms that your tank can accommodate). One that I've read or heard many times is, you can safely keep two inches of fish length for every ten gallons of tank volume–or something to that effect. According to this rule, our model 55-gallon aquarium can accommodate approximately 11 inches of fish length.

The trouble is, this rule overlooks some very important factors, such as the overall height and thickness of a fish's body, its feeding habits, and, by logical extension, how much waste it produces. The bottom line is, total body length doesn't really tell you much about the impact a fish or community of fish will have on your aquarium's biological filter. By means of illustration, one 11-inch Picasso triggerfish (*Rhinecanthus aculeatus*), which is a relatively greedy and sloppy carnivore, will place considerably more of a burden on your biofilter than will a small school of two-inch cardinalfish (family Apogonidae). My suggestion is to use the 2-inches-per-every-ten-gallons rule as a basic guideline only. Beyond that, a little common sense combined with the knowledge you've already acquired about the fish you intend to keep will help you to make sound, educated stocking decisions.

In some ways, stocking a marine aquarium is more art than science. Start by introducing only two or three hardy specimens, and wait a few weeks to see how they adjust before adding more fish. If all goes well during that time, go ahead and introduce some more specimens, one at a time, testing diligently for ammonia and nitrite after each introduction. If you're adding specimens at the proper rate, the population of nitrifying bacteria should grow proportionally in response to the increasing biological load, and, therefore, no ammonia or nitrite should be detected.

As you add specimens to the aquarium, you'll notice that each fish will claim a certain area within the tank for its territory. One might stake out a cave in the rockwork. Another might dig a burrow in the substrate. Still another might routinely perch on a small ledge or outcropping, waiting for food items to float past. By carefully observing the interaction between the different fish, you should be able to approximate where one territory ends and another begins. Why is this important? Because an aquarium's carrying capacity is not just based on the population of nitrifying bacteria. Available "real estate" plays a major role as well. Once all of the available territories have been claimed, any further additions of fish may prove problematic, even if the biological filter is capable of handling more waste material.

Territoriality and the new fish on the block

Inclusiveness is not a high priority among most reef fish, and oftentimes, even when there is plenty of space left in the aquarium to accommodate additional specimens, a newcomer will be ruthlessly harassed by one or more of the established fish in the community. In some cases, this may be because the newcomer is simply too similar in habit or appearance to the aggressor fish, in which case, the best way to resolve the dispute is to return the new fish to the dealer and make a different selection. But in other cases, you might be able to diffuse the aggression simply by rearranging the rockwork and decorations prior to introducing the new fish, thereby disrupting the established territories. The theory behind this approach is that the established fish will no longer feel like they have "home tank advantage," and they'll have to focus their attention on finding new territories rather than tormenting the newcomer. Sometimes it works; sometimes it doesn't.

For clownfish, their anemone is their territory.

Acclimating your new fish

Typically, your dealer will package your newly purchased fish in plastic bags filled with oxygenated aquarium water for the journey home. But you can't simply dump the fish and water out of their bags and into your new

Acclimate your new fish carefully.

Sphaeramia nematoptera, the pajama cardinalfish, is an easy-going fish and hardy as well.

aquarium once you get them home. First, you have to acclimate the fish to the water conditions in your aquarium, which will undoubtedly differ considerably from the water conditions in your dealer's tanks. Of course, if you intend to isolate your new fish properly, you'll need to acclimate them to the water in the quarantine tank first, but since the water parameters should be the same between your display tank and quarantine tank (and for the sake of brevity), we won't worry about making that distinction here.

In years past, the commonly accepted practice for acclimating fish was to float the bag containing the fish in the new aquarium for about a half hour to give it an opportunity to adjust to the change in water temperature. A major drawback to this method was that it didn't give the fish a chance to become acclimated to the other water parameters–pH, specific gravity, etc.–before being released into its new surroundings. Also, the original water was typically dumped right into the new aquarium along with any pollutants, parasites, or pathogens that might have been present in the dealer's tanks.

A better technique is to pour the fish and the original water gently from the bag into a separate plastic container. You might want to have some sort of makeshift cover handy in case the fish decides to jump. Next, begin to add small quantities of aquarium water to the container, every 15 minutes or so, until the temperature, pH, and specific gravity of the water in the plastic container are the same as in the aquarium. Then, net the fish out of the container and release it immediately into the aquarium. It's a good idea to thoroughly moisten the net in aquarium water ahead of time to minimize any trauma to the fish's body.

The first few weeks after acclimation and release will be a critical period of adjustment for your new fish. They won't be able to tell you whether they are being harassed constantly by their tankmates or that their dietary needs are not being fulfilled properly. It's up to you to monitor your new charges closely and to correct any problems that might develop before they get out of hand. It's also during this stressful adjustment period that disease or parasitic infection is most likely to occur, but if you continue to maintain excellent water quality and stable conditions overall, problems stemming from disease or parasites can be minimized.

Dealing with the "hunger strike"

Try not to be alarmed if a newly introduced fish refuses to eat for several days after arriving in its new home. This is a fairly common response, and it's understandable when you consider the cumulative stress a wild-caught fish has to undergo from the point of collection until it arrives in your aquarium. Essentially, each fish is netted and removed from its home on the coral reef, sent overseas in a bag full of less-than-pristine water, retained temporarily in a holding facility tank, shipped on to a hectic aquarium shop where it is placed in a display tank. From there, the fish is netted yet again and transported to an aquarist's home where it is acclimated to different water conditions for the umpteenth time and then offered an assortment of unfamiliar food items. It's not surprising, then, that a fish might be a little reluctant to eat. Most people I know wouldn't eat under those circumstances either!

Large, predatory fish will make a fine meal of earthworms.

It is a rare non-aquarist who can correctly feed your fish in your absence. Fish can easily go two weeks without being fed.

Do not ask a non-aquarist friend to feed your fish for you while you are on vacation. If you will be gone for more than two weeks, either enlist the help of a hobbyist friend or, if you have to rely on a non-aquarist, pre-portion the amounts to be fed on a daily basis—and then hide your regular food supply. The exception to the rule that your fish can go up to two weeks without feeding is with young fry.

If you are raising tanks of fry, however, you will no longer be a beginner, and you'll be able to make appropriate arrangements.

Part 3

Brine shrimp are perpetual favorites.

Given a little time to adjust, most marine fish will begin to accept standard flake, freeze-dried, or frozen foods within two or three days. However, a fish that continues to "hunger strike" much beyond this may need to be enticed with some live foods. Smaller fish can generally be coaxed with items like live adult brine shrimp or bloodworms, while larger predatory fish can often be brought around with larger shrimp, crayfish, or earthworms. Feeder fish can also be offered to larger piscivores if nothing else seems to be working, but I would strongly caution you to feed them sparingly and to wean your fish off them as soon as possible. Feeder fish are problematic for several reasons, which we will examine in greater detail in the chapter on feeding.

Another method that is often successful in getting new fish to feed is to attach a strip of fresh fish or clam to the end of a feeding stick (available at any aquarium shop) and give it a little jiggle in front of the fish. The movement seems to send the message that the food item is alive, and the smell of fresh seafood permeating the water often proves irresistible to even the most stubborn fish. Not surprisingly, you can use this same technique to wean a large predatory fish off feeders.

Selecting Invertebrates for the Mini-reef

For the uninitiated reef aquarist, choosing healthy sessile invertebrates for the mini-reef can be something of a challenge. This is due largely to the fact that it's often difficult to know exactly what a healthy invertebrate is supposed to look like. To a certain degree, most of us can recognize an ailing fish. We might not be able to identify the exact cause or nature of the illness, but we can usually tell that something is wrong if a fish behaves in a peculiar fashion or has strange spots or growths somewhere on its body. But how is a sessile invertebrate supposed to look and behave?

Signs of a healthy sessile invertebrate

As when purchasing fish, the first thing you'll want to look at when selecting invertebrates is the

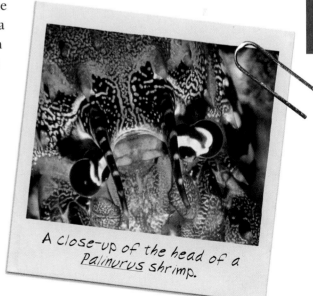

A close-up of the head of a Palinurus shrimp.

Pagurus sp., one of the hermit crabs.

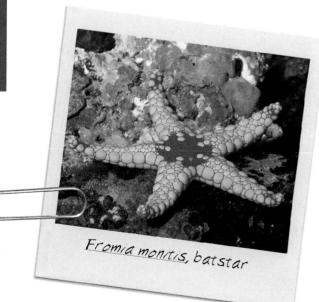

Fromia monitis, batstar

condition of the dealer's tanks. Are they choked with algae or detritus and reeking of decomposition? Are the inverts packed extremely close together? Are the tanks poorly lit? If any of these conditions applies to your dealer's tanks, your best bet is to shop elsewhere. Invertebrates kept under such conditions will most likely be in poor health and will gradually waste away in your aquarium.

Next, carefully examine the bodies of the invertebrates themselves. There should be no signs of tissue damage anywhere on the animals, as it can lead to bacterial infection and ultimately death. Pay special attention to the fleshy base of each animal or colony of animals to make sure it has not been injured during collection. Such injuries commonly lead to the rapid deterioration of the invertebrate. A healthy specimen will be attached firmly to a rock, the aquarium glass, or the substrate. Specimens attached to small, portable rocks are preferable because it's easier to transfer them from tank to tank without the risk of injuring the base. Also, examine each animal for discolored lesions, powdery-looking areas, or slimy patches, which can be an indication of disease.

Healthy anemones and polyps should contract rapidly when disturbed but should remain fully expanded at most other times. Tubeworms should withdraw their feathery feeding tentacles into their tubes whenever they feel threatened, which is virtually any time they detect sudden movement either inside or outside their aquarium. Stony corals should be fully expanded with no evidence of decay or damage on their soft tissues. Also, avoid any stony coral specimens that appear to be receding or pulling away from their calcium carbonate skeletons.

It's extremely helpful to examine color photographs of the invertebrates you'd like to keep before heading for the aquarium shop. That way, you'll have a better idea of how healthy specimens are supposed to look. Being familiar with natural coloration is especially important when selecting photosynthetic invertebrates that get their color from the symbiotic zooxanthellae residing in their tissues. When these invertebrates are ill or under stress, they'll often shed their zooxanthellae, causing them to lose their natural coloration and giving them a bleached appearance. Once they lose their zooxanthellae, these invertebrates are generally a lost cause in the

Lysmata debelius, the blood shrimp, is much coveted for the mini-reef.

What to look for when buying sessile invertebrates

It can be extremely challenging for the novice reef aquarist to distinguish between a healthy sessile invertebrate and an ailing one. Here are some signs to look for:

• Specimens are displayed in a well-maintained, algae-free aquarium.

There is no evidence of injury, tissue damage, or decay.

• Corals and anemones contract their tentacles rapidly when disturbed but are fully extended otherwise.

• Tridacnid clams have healthy-looking mantles that are not receding from the shell and snap shut when disturbed.

• Tubeworms have a full complement of feeding/respiratory tentacles that quickly withdraw into their tubes at any sudden movement.

• Animals exhibit their natural coloration (i.e., they donít look pale or bleached).

• The dealer demonstrates knowledge of proper handling/bagging techniques and can vouch for the fact that the animal has never been exposed to air.

This is the red serpent seastar.

Linckia laevigata, the blue linckia, needs a mature tank with algae and lots of hiding places.

aquarium, so having a color photo as a basis for comparison will help you avoid buying specimens that may already be in decline.

Selecting motile invertebrates

Thus far, we've focused primarily on sessile invertebrates for the reef tank, but there is also a vast array of beautiful and exotic motile invertebrates, including various crustaceans, echinoderms, and mollusks, that are often suitable for both mini-reef and fish-only aquariums. When purchasing motile invertebrates, you should be concerned mostly with selecting specimens that are completely intact and moving actively about the tank in pursuit of food items. Lethargic specimens should be avoided as a general rule, but keep in mind that some are nocturnal and may be inactive during daylight hours.

Crabs, shrimp, and other crustaceans will attempt to evade capture by hiding amidst the rockwork or behind decorations, a source of aggravation for the shopkeeper, but a general indication of good health. You can also tell a lot about a crustacean's state of health by examining its mouthparts. If they aren't perpetually in motion, you should pass on the specimen because it is probably ill. Don't worry if a crustacean is missing a single claw or leg as long as it seems to be in good condition otherwise. The missing limb will be replaced when the animal molts (sheds its exoskeleton) again.

Determining the health of an echinoderm, such as a seastar, sea cucumber, or sea urchin, can be a little trickier, since many of them are extremely slow moving by nature.

Part 3

Brittlestars, which are capable of surprisingly rapid bursts of speed, are an exception. Seastars should be plump and firm with no sunken tissue on their central disks or along the margin of their arms. When disturbed, their tube feet should retract slowly but consistently. Sea cucumbers and the closely related sea apples should also be firm to the touch and plump, and they should retract their feeding tentacles promptly when bothered. Urchins should have a full complement of erect spines, and their tube feet should be in motion.

Snails, including the algae-munching turbo snails, and other univalve mollusks should have complete, undamaged shells, and they should be active in the dealer's tank. Of course, given the relatively slow pace of many univalves, you may need to spend several minutes observing a particular specimen before you can make a judgment concerning its health. Bivalves, such as the brilliantly colored flame scallop (*Lima scabra*) and the ever-popular tridacnid clams, should snap their shells closed when disturbed. Otherwise, their siphons should be visible and their mantels should be fully expanded.

Compatibility among sessile invertebrates

We've already discussed the importance of selecting compatible fish species for inclusion in your new marine aquarium. But what about sessile invertebrates? Is it possible that they, too, can make life miserable for one another? The answer is a resounding "yes!" The only difference is, the methods employed by certain invertebrates to keep their neighbors from encroaching on their individual territories are far more insidious than anything the average aquarium fish can inflict on its enemies.

For example, many coral species, such as the beautiful yet potent bubble corals (*Plerogyra sinuosa*) and elegance corals (*Catalaphyllia jardinei*), will ruthlessly sting neighboring invertebrates with their long feeding tentacles. Some also sting with specialized

Brittlestars have visible spines on their arms, while serpent stars do not.

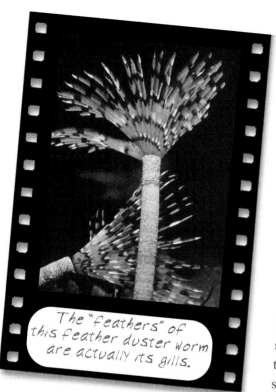

The "feathers" of this feather duster worm are actually its gills.

Part 3

"sweeper" tentacles that are capable of extending well beyond the reach of their feeding tentacles. Several of the stony corals, especially members of the *Euphyllia* genus (e.g., frogspawn corals and vase corals), are equipped with these sweeper tentacles and are ready, willing, and able to put them to use to defend their territories in the aquarium. Because this stinging behavior typically occurs after "lights out," it generally goes unobserved by the aquarist. On the other hand, it's hard to miss the injuries they inflict.

Preventing stinging deaths and injuries is a simple matter of spacing out your invertebrates properly. As a general rule, the space between two invertebrates should be approximately equal to the diameter of the larger species at maturity. This should provide ample room for each animal to grow to full size without coming into contact with its neighbors. However, certain rapid-growing corals may need to be "pruned back" routinely to keep them within reasonable boundaries.

Sea anemones are also prone to stinging their neighbors especially when that neighbor happens to be another anemone. Unlike corals, anemones have the capacity to detach themselves and move about the aquarium to attack a perceived intruder. While these aggressive forays are seldom directed at corals or other sessile invertebrates, they may accidentally blunder into contact with them, causing injury nonetheless. Because anemones are mobile and have the propensity to sting fellow anemones, they should be kept one to a tank. It's also best to introduce an

Territoriality among sessile invertebrates

Don't let their sedentary lifestyles fool you. Many sessile invertebrates are completely capable of waging war on their neighbors when they perceive that their territories are being invaded. Some of their more sinister methods include:

• Rapidly overgrowing and shading out the competition

• Ruthlessly stinging interlopers with their feeding tentacles

• Mobilizing on search-and-destroy missions (anemones)

• Launching nocturnal long-range strikes with specialized "sweeper tentacles"

• Coral chemical warfare, the release of chemical compounds, called terpenoids, to inhibit the growth of encroaching neighbors.

anemone before any other invertebrates in a mini-reef. That way, it has an opportunity to settle into its own little niche before competition arrives.

Some corals, including the leather corals (*Sarcophyton spp.*) and the pulse corals (*Xenia spp.*), may actually wage a form of chemical warfare on their tankmates. That is, they are capable of releasing toxic compounds (called terpenoids) into the water to discourage predation and to inhibit the growth of neighboring corals. On the coral reef, these compounds are quickly diluted by ocean water. However, terpenoids can have a major impact in the closed system of the aquarium where dilution is minimal. In some instances, the release of these compounds can actually cause the death of every coral in the aquarium. To help facilitate the removal of terpenoids from the system, be sure to utilize a high-quality protein skimmer. It's also helpful to maintain a good amount of water movement throughout the aquarium, so these compounds cannot accumulate among your invertebrates as readily.

Acclimating invertebrates

As with introducing new fish, invertebrates must also be carefully acclimated to the water conditions in their new home. In fact, gradual acclimation is even more critical for sessile invertebrates than it is for many fish species, as their delicate tissues can be damaged easily by a rapid change in specific gravity (osmotic shock). Rushing the process almost invariably leads to ailing or dying specimens.

Sea cucumbers are holothurians that live on the sandy sea floor.

copulating nudibranchs.

The feather duster worm, Sabellastarte magnifica.

In the previous chapter, I suggested acclimating marine fish in a separate plastic container in order to minimize the potential of introducing pathogens or parasites that might be present in your dealer's water to your new aquarium. However, this method is highly impractical for acclimating sessile invertebrates primarily because there's no good way to transfer them from the plastic container to the aquarium without completely removing them from the water. When exposed to air, many sessile invertebrates (as well as certain echinoderms) can get air trapped in their tissues, ultimately leading to death, so they must be kept fully submerged at all times. This rule should be observed from the moment your dealer bags the specimens for you until they are released into your new aquarium.

That being said, let's get back to the acclimation process. Float the plastic bag containing the invertebrate in your new aquarium for at least 15 minutes so the specimen can adjust to the temperature difference. Then, open the top of the bag to allow air to enter, and trickle in a small quantity of aquarium water. Every five minutes or so, add more aquarium water to the bag until the pH and specific gravity are equalized. I find it convenient to drape the open end of the bag over the side of the tank to keep it from filling with aquarium water too quickly. Also, you can gently rest the lid of your aquarium hood (if one is used) on the open end of the bag to keep it stationary. Continue the process for a minimum of 30 minutes (for a total acclimation time of around 45 minutes). Once you've finished acclimating the specimen, gently remove the animal while the bag is submerged, and place it in a predetermined location in the aquarium. Do not dump the water from the bag into the aquarium. Carefully lift the bag out of the tank, with the open end facing up, and dump the water down the drain. A small amount of the original water might be released when you transfer the animal into the aquarium, but most will be retained in the bag.

Keep in mind that when introducing sessile invertebrates, there's more to consider than just acclimating them to different water parameters. It's very important to do a little "homework" before buying specimens so you know ahead of time how they should be

Part 3

placed in the aquarium. For example, photosynthetic species, especially the highly light-sensitive stony corals, should be positioned high on the rockwork where they can derive the greatest benefit from the high-intensity lighting system. Less light-sensitive coral and anemone species can be placed lower down as can tubeworms, which have no special lighting requirement.

Fish in the mini-reef

Many reef aquarists prefer to avoid including fish in their setups altogether, due to the fact that their waste products tend to degrade water quality and because it can be next to impossible to capture and remove a sick or dead fish from a mini-reef system. There are simply too many convenient "bolt holes" and hiding places in a mini-reef to allow for easy netting. It's also undesirable to attempt to medicate an ailing fish in a mini-reef aquarium because many of the medications suitable for treating fish diseases are highly toxic to invertebrates and should only be administered in a separate quarantine tank. But in spite of the risks, some reefkeepers prefer the natural look of a mini-reef that contains a few carefully chosen fish.

Count 'em in

In order for a fish to be a desirable candidate for the mini-reef, it must not put too much of a strain on the biofilter with its eating habits and waste and must not include sessile invertebrates as a routine part of its diet. For example, the wildly colored and patterned mandarinfish (*Synchiropus splendidus*) and the aptly named psychedelic fish (*S. picturatus*) are both terrific candidates for the mini-reef, both being extremely shy and retiring, and feeding primarily on tiny crustaceans that emerge from live rock. The diminutive clownfish and damsels (family Pomacentridae) are also well suited to life in the mini-reef. One or two clownfish would be especially fascinating if paired with an appropriate host anemone. It's best to keep only one damsel in a mini-reef, however, to avoid the warfare that

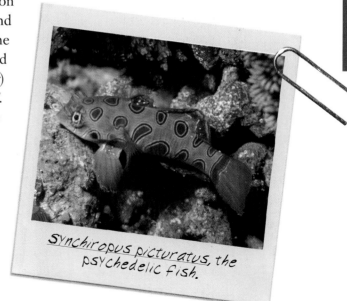

Synchiropus picturatus, the psychedelic fish.

Part 3

Percula clownfish are widely captive bred and raised

Part 3

A sampler of reef-friendly marine fish

Clownfish and damsels (family Pomacentridae)

Basslets and dottybacks (family Pseudochromidae)

Fairy basslets (family Grammidae)

Cardinalfish (family Apogonidae)

Dragonets (family Callionymidae)

Anthias (family Serranidae)

Blennies (family Blenniidae)

Gobies (family Gobiidae)

Hawkfish (family Cirrhitidae)

Firefish (family Microdesmidae)

Dwarf angelfish (family Pomacanthidae)

invariably erupts when two or more are kept together. Several species of basslet and dottyback (family Pseudochromidae) are also suitable for the mini-reef, provided they are kept singly. Like the damsels, basslets and dottybacks can be extremely territorial and pugnacious with conspecifics, and their aggression may extend to any other fish that is similar in coloration or body shape. The various cardinalfish (family Apogonidae) are also generally well behaved in the mini-reef, and you can usually house several together in the same tank quite peacefully.

Of course, this is just a small sampling of the fish species that are suitable for inclusion in a reef tank. With a little guidance from a trusted dealer, you should be able to assemble a small group of fish that are uniquely attractive and fascinating to observe without harming the invertebrates or heavily impacting the water quality in your mini-reef. But remember, the key to success when combining sessile inverts and fish in the same tank is to choose your fish according to the needs of the invertebrates, not the other way around.

Count 'em out

On the flipside of the coin, there are various fish species that should be excluded from the mini-reef with prejudice. For example, most species of triggerfish (family Balistidae) are totally unsuitable because they feed on invertebrates. Often, they'll just sample a potential food item to determine whether it's worth eating, but because triggers have such impressive dentition, even curious nibbling can cause considerable damage or death. Another drawback to keeping triggerfish in the mini-reef is that your chances of catching and removing a sick or troublesome specimen are virtually nil. When a trigger sees a net coming, it will simply lock itself into a crevice in the rockwork with its locking dorsal spine, making extraction extremely difficult.

Butterflyfish (family Chaetodontidae) are also problematic in the mini-reef, as most species routinely include coral polyps and anemones in their diets. Unless you want to offer up your prized invertebrates as an incredibly extravagant smorgasbord, it's best to pass on the butterflyfish. One possible exception is the copperband butterflyfish (*Chelmon rostratus*), which is sometimes introduced to devour invasive aiptasia anemones that occasionally stowaway in the mini-reef on live rock. But even this relatively innocuous species will sometimes turn its attention toward valued invertebrates.

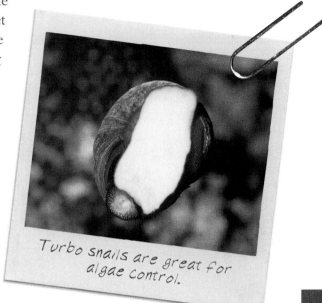

Turbo snails are great for algae control.

The parrotfish (family Scaridae) are another group of coral munchers that are best left out of the mini-reef. Their natural diet consists mainly of algae-encrusted coral heads, which they chomp into reef rubble with their tough, beak-like mouths. In fact, much of the coarse sand substrate surrounding coral reefs is actually produced by the grinding mouths of parrotfish. Apart from their destructive feeding habits, most species of parrotfish become much too large for the average mini-reef (not to mention the average fish-only aquarium).

Again, this is only a partial list of fish that are undesirable for inclusion in a reef aquarium. As a general rule, if you have any uncertainty about the behavior, feeding habits, or ultimate

Limpet.

Part 3

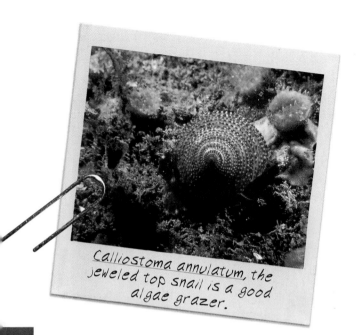

Calliostoma annulatum, the jeweled top snail is a good algae grazer.

size of a particular species of fish, in other words, it you aren't absolutely certain that the fish has a proven record of being safe around invertebrates, it's best to leave it out of your mini-reef.

Some Excellent Beginner Fish

If you're like most people making their first foray into marine fishkeeping, you're hoping to establish a peaceful, yet lively, community of hardy and colorful specimens. But how do you know which species to start off with? Fortunately, there's quite a diversity of resilient marine fish that are perfectly suited for the beginner's tank, many of which are strikingly beautiful to boot! While there's no realistic way to chronicle every single marine fish that is desirable to beginners, there are several noteworthy examples that justify a closer look.

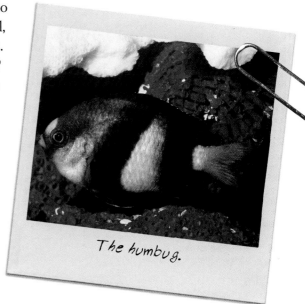

The humbug.

The damsels

When it comes to tolerating the fluctuating water parameters that sometimes prevail in beginners' aquariums, no other group of fish can compare to

Chromis viridis, the blue-green damsel.

the damsels (family Pomacentridae). These fish have several advantages that make them the ideal first fish for the novice marine aquarist. For one thing, they seldom grow larger than 3-4 inches in captivity, and they will readily accept all standard aquarium fare, including flake, freeze-dried, frozen, and live foods. Damsels also come in a wide range of dazzling colors, from the stark, contrasting white and black bands of the humbug damsel (*Dascyllus aruanus*) to the royal blue and bright yellow of the yellow-tailed blue damsel (*Chromis xanthuras*) to the iridescent green-blue of the green chromis (*Chromis caerulea*).

The only drawback to this hardy and forgiving group of fish is that they can be extremely territorial and feisty toward their tankmates, especially toward other damsels. However, there are some simple steps you can take to help reduce their aggression. For one thing, avoid keeping more than one damsel of any given species in the same tank. Otherwise, protracted territorial disputes are virtually unavoidable. Exceptions can sometimes be made if the fish are housed in a very large tank with ample hiding places. It's also helpful to introduce the damsel after all the other specimens have had a chance to establish territories. That way, the damsel will be the "new fish on the block" and won't be as likely to view the other fish as intruders. In the event that a damsel has already established its territory, and you'd like to introduce some additional fish, you can sometimes avert conflict by rearranging the rockwork ahead of time to disrupt the defined territorial boundaries.

The clownfish (anemonefish)

Close cousins to the damsels, the various clownfish species (another group of Pomacentrids) are also excellent beginner fish. Owing to their famous symbiotic relationship with anemones, clownfish have, perhaps, influenced more people to become involved in the marine aquarium hobby than any other marine animal. In fact, it was the common clownfish (*Amphiprion ocellaris*) that first enticed me into marine fishkeeping. You may not be familiar with this fish by its scientific name, but you'd undoubtedly recognize one if you saw it. For many marine aquarists, *A. ocellaris*, with its comical antics and its

Part 3

almost surreal orange, white, and black coloration, is the consummate clownfish. The percula clownfish (*Amphiprion percula*) sports coloration and pattering that are nearly identical to *A. ocellaris*. The only difference is, the percula clownfish has slightly more pronounced black markings on its body and fins. Both species make equally delightful additions to the beginner's aquarium. Other excellent choices include the maroon clownfish (*Premnas biaculeatus*), Clark's clownfish (*Amphiprion clarkii*), and the tomato clownfish (*Amphiprion frenatus*).

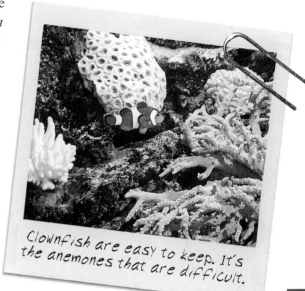

Clownfish are easy to keep. It's the anemones that are difficult.

In spite of the fact that they seek refuge among the stinging tentacles of anemones in the wild, clownfish can be kept quite satisfactorily in captivity without an anemone. This is good news for newcomers to the hobby. While clownfish are relatively easy to keep, the same cannot be said for anemones. Even advanced reef aquarists have a hard time providing the exacting water conditions that are necessary to keep anemones alive in captivity for any length of time. If you're new to the aquarium hobby in general and are considering keeping a clownfish and anemone together, I would strongly urge you to reconsider the anemone, at least for now. You can always add one later on after you've gotten a little more experience under your belt.

Like the closely related damsels, territorial aggression can be a problem with certain clownfish species. In the case of my own percula clownfish, this aggression seems to be directed only at my hand whenever I'm performing some routine maintenance task in the aquarium. The little bugger ruthlessly nips at my fingers whenever I get too close to its little cave between the rockwork and substrate. Otherwise, it seems to

Amphiprion sandaracinos is commensal with the anemones, *Stoichactis giganteum* and *S. mertensii*.

Large and delicate, marine angels like the emperor angel, are not for beginners.

get along just fine with its tankmates, one of which happens to be a yellow-tailed blue damsel. If clownfish territoriality should become a problem, you can generally overcome it, using the same techniques as described above for damsels.

The dwarf angels

Unlike the full-sized marine angelfish (the emperor angel, queen angel, French angel, etc.), which generally are considered too delicate for the beginner's aquarium, several dwarf (or pygmy) angels of the *Centropyge* genus (family Pomacanthidae) are terrific choices for the novice aquarist. These fish reach a very manageable size of only around four inches at maturity, and they adapt readily to aquarium conditions. Dwarf angels can be trained to accept a wide range of food items, including most standard flake, freeze-dried, and frozen foods, but most species also require a good amount of algae in their diets, which can be provided in the form of dried marine algae. Of particular interest to beginner aquarists are the coral beauty *(Centropyge bispinosus)*, the lemonpeel angelfish *(Centropyge flavissimus)*, and the flame angelfish *(Centropyge loriculus)*.

The coral beauty is an absolute delight to behold. The head and body of this exceedingly well-behaved dwarf angel are a bluish-purple. Its flanks are gold or reddish-gold interrupted by a series of vertical purple stripes. The fins are blue to purplish blue, with the exception of the pectoral fins, which are transparent yellow. And this description hardly does justice to the coral beauty's coloration. In fact, there are subtle distinctions in coloration between individuals, depending on the location from which they were collected. You really have to see this fish to believe it.

Centropyge loriculus, the flame angel.

The aptly named lemonpeel angelfish is almost totally bright yellow in color, which really makes this fish "pop" in the average community aquarium. The only variation from this monochrome is a light blue ring around each eye, a small blue streak on the edges of its gill covers, and an almost imperceptible pinkish tint on the outer margins of its dorsal, caudal, and anal fins. The lemonpeel angelfish is predominately a grazer, so don't hold back on the greens.

Centropyge flavissimus, the lemonpeel angel.

The flame angelfish gets its name from its dramatic orange-red overall coloration. Along its flanks are five or six dark vertical bands. The margins of its dorsal, caudal, and anal fins are tinged with blue. Like the lemon peel angelfish, the flame angelfish's vivid color really makes it stand out from the rest of the fish in a community tank. This fish is just slightly more demanding when it comes to water quality than the other two dwarf angels we've discussed, but it shares their peaceful demeanor and willingness to accept a wide range of food items.

Each of these three species is commonly available at most marine aquarium shops (at a fairly reasonable price, I might add). Though they are relatively peaceful, they generally will not tolerate conspecifics and may square off with other species that are very similar in size, shape, or color.

The hawkfish

If you're looking for small, peaceful fish with a little character and personality for your community, you can't go wrong with the various hawkfish (family Cirrhitidae). These fish get their name not so much from their appearance, but rather from their habit of perching on coral outcroppings and swooping down on prey items as they swim by or drift past in the current. Because they lack swimbladders, they are generally poor swimmers and spend most of their time resting on the rockwork, propped up on their pectoral fins. When they choose to move, they typically get around by hopping comically from rock to rock.

The feature that is most appealing about hawkfish is their apparent awareness of

Part 3

Centropyge bispinosus, the coral beauty angel.

The scarlet hawkfish.

everything that goes on around them. Their large, high-set eyes are always glancing about, keeping track of all the activity both inside and outside the tank. They'll even follow the aquarist with their eyes once they figure out from whom their "daily bread" comes.

Hawkfish are predatory by nature and should be offered plenty of meaty foods in the aquarium. They'll gladly accept most live, frozen, and freeze-dried foods and will even learn to accept flake food over time. The only food they'll completely ignore is marine algae and other greens. If you offer these items to a hawkfish, it will merely roll its eyes at you and flash you a little fishy expression that seems to say, "You don't honestly expect me to eat this, do you?"

The three most commonly sold hawkfish species are the scarlet (or flame) hawkfish _(Neocirrhites armatus)_, the longnosed hawkfish _(Oxycirrhites typus)_, and the pixy hawkfish _(Cirrhitichthys oxycephalus)_, although other species sometimes make their way into dealers' tanks as well. The scarlet hawkfish is, perhaps, the most popular and attractive of the three, with its short, blunt body and its intense (you guessed it!) scarlet coloration. Unfortunately, since the supply of this fish is relatively short and the demand is relatively high, the scarlet hawkfish is the most expensive of the three.

The longnosed hawkfish has a more elongated body than the scarlet hawkfish, and, as the name suggests, it has a long pointy snout. The snout is perfectly designed for reaching into tight crevices on the coral reef for tiny crustaceans and other food items. Its overall coloration is white with a repeating square pattern made up of bright red lines. At the tip of each dorsal spine are little hair-like appendages called cirrhi, which are not as pronounced on the scarlet hawkfish.

My favorite of the three commonly sold hawkfish species is the pixy hawkfish. With its stocky body and short snout, this fish is closer in body shape to the scarlet hawkfish, but it is more similar in coloration to the longnosed hawkfish. Instead of a box pattern, it has dark rust-colored blotches ringed with orange against a white background. Cirrhi are also clearly visible on the dorsal spines of this species.

The yellow tang

Most tangs and surgeonfish (family Acanthuridae) are touchy when it comes to water quality and diet, making them better suited for experienced aquarists than for beginners. And this is a real shame, since many of them are just drop-dead gorgeous. My personal favorite is the regal tang (*Paracanthurus hepatus*) with its stunning blue body, black "painter's pallet" side markings, and bright yellow tail. Unfortunately, when I attempted to keep one of these fish in my first marine aquarium (before I knew anything about their specific dietary requirements and their need for near-pristine water conditions) it contracted a disease and wasted away in short order.

My own personal catastrophes aside, one particular species of tang, the yellow tang (*Zebrasoma flavescens*), is fairly forgiving and will thrive under conditions that would not be tolerated by most tangs and surgeons. This is not

The longnosed hawkfish.

The yellow tang.

Part 3

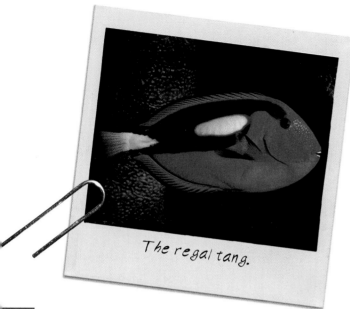

The regal tang.

to suggest that it can tolerate neglect or wildly fluctuating water parameters. On the contrary, it will likely become ill and perish if there are too many dissolved organic compounds in the water. A good protein skimmer is highly recommended if you intend to keep this species, and, of course, it's important to keep up with those water changes. Also, since they are naturally found in relatively shallow water where wave action is heavy, they require highly oxygenated water and ample water movement such as that provided by a strong powerhead.

Like all tangs and surgeons, the yellow tang has an extremely laterally compressed body and a scalpel-like spine on its caudal peduncle (the base of the tail). The spine can be erected, in switchblade-like fashion, whenever the fish feels threatened, so care must be taken when netting these fish. However, you don't have to worry about being attacked and injured by one of these fish whenever you place your hand in the aquarium. It will simply flee to the opposite end of the tank or hide within the rockwork when it sees your hand approaching. Yellow tangs are territorial with their own or similar species, but they are very peaceful otherwise.

Tangs and surgeons are herbivores, preferring to graze throughout the day on algae, and the yellow tang is no exception. In order to keep this fish in good health, you must provide ample greens on a daily basis. Avoid feeding lettuce, spinach, and other terrestrial greens, as they cannot be digested properly. Instead, offer dried nori (the seaweed used to wrap sushi) or red marine algae. Both contain the necessary nutrients for marine organisms and will be accepted with enthusiasm.

The "scalpel" can be seen near the tail of this yellow tang.

What's with the scientific names?

You may be wondering why I list the scientific name of each fish or invertebrate species in parentheses after its common name. The reason is, relying on common names when choosing animals for your marine aquarium can create lots of confusion and may even lead to disaster. Take the common name "powder brown tang" for example. You will find that two very similar looking species, *Acanthurus nigricans* and *Acanthurus japonicus*, are both sold under this common name. They are so similar in appearance, in fact, that the layman would have a very difficult time telling them apart without seeing both species side-by-side. The only problem is, *A. nigricans* doesn't adapt well to life in captivity and usually dies within a few weeks of purchase, while *A. japonicus* is remarkably well-suited for the aquarium.

And this is only one example out of many. In some cases, the same common name is used to describe three or more different species, all of which might have radically different care requirements. The bottom line is, if you arm yourself with the scientific names of the various marine organisms that interest you before heading for the aquarium store, you'll be sure to get the exact species you're after.

As I suggested at the beginning of this chapter, this by no means exhausts the list of marine fish that are suitable for the novice aquarist. Your dealer will, no doubt, be able to expand upon this list considerably and help you select a peaceful, compatible community of fish that will bring you years of pleasure.

A Sampler of Troublesome Fish

Okay, we've taken a good look at some species of marine fish that make great additions to the beginner's aquarium, but that's only part of the picture. When shopping for your first specimens, you'll undoubtedly come across species that are irresistibly beautiful or exotic-looking but don't really belong in the average novice aquarist's tank. In fact, some commonly sold species aren't suitable for any aquarium, regardless of how experienced the aquarist might be.

Keep your hands to yourself!

The first group of potentially troublesome fish consists of the various and sundry venomous species that are frequently offered for sale. By venomous, I mean any fish capable of inflicting a painful toxic

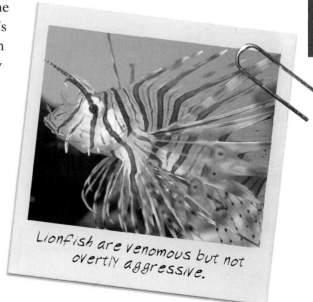

Lionfish are venomous but not overtly aggressive.

He's as bad as he looks. This stonefish is dangerous!

The bicolor foxface has a painful sting.

sting through sharp spines on its body. The different species of lionfish (family Scorpaenidae) all fall into this category, and they are widely available in the aquarium trade. In fact, I don't recall ever being in a marine aquarium shop that didn't have at least one lionfish (usually *Pterois volitans*) for sale.

A lionfish's sting, which is delivered by its beautiful, flowing, hypodermic-like dorsal spines, is not usually deadly, but it can cause excruciating pain. Many who have been stung compare the pain to that inflicted by a bee or wasp sting. Another drawback to lionfish is that they can engulf any fish small enough to fit into their cavernous mouths and so are best kept alone in a large species tank.

Lionfish are generally non-aggressive (except to their prey items) and will not actively seek to sting an aquarist. More often than not, a sting results from accidentally brushing up against the fish while performing routine maintenance tasks in the tank. Some unwitting aquarists have even been stung through the plastic bag used to transport the fish home from the aquarium shop. Also, the fact that many lionfish and other Scorpaenids have very cryptic coloration makes it easy to lose track of their location in the tank and, hence, to make inadvertent contact. Should you get stung by one of these fish, you can break down the highly unstable venom and help alleviate the pain by soaking the affected body part (usually the hand) in very hot water.

Speaking of cryptic coloration, one relative of the lionfish that is completely inappropriate for the novice aquarist, and, indeed, for most advanced aquarists, is the extremely venomous stonefish (*Synanceia horrida*) along with its highly toxic kin *S. trachynis* and *S. verrucosa*. These fish sport such outstanding camouflage that you can look right at them without discerning the outline of a fish. They're also armed with sharp dorsal spines capable of delivering a highly toxic venom that can cause intense pain, paralysis, and even death, depending on how many spines penetrate the skin of the unfortunate aquarist. Under no circumstances should one of these species be kept in a home where curious youngsters might be tempted to put their hands into the aquarium. The potential for tragedy is just too great.

The various foxfaces, including *Lo vulpinus, Lo uspi,* and *Lo magnifica* (all members of the Siganidae family), are also venomous species that often make their way into dealer's tanks. Generally, these unassuming grazers are very peaceful with their tankmates but possess dorsal and anal spines capable of inflicting a painful sting. As with the various lionfish, the foxfaces do not use their venomous spines offensively. Stings usually occur through accidental contact while netting or transporting one of these fish or while maintaining the aquarium.

A shoal of juvenile saltwater catfish (*Plotosus lineatus*) is a delight to behold in the wild. The young congregate together in tight defensive "balls" that seem to roll comically along the ocean floor whenever they feel threatened. Unfortunately, this behavior seldom manifests itself in captivity unless a large number of these fish are kept together. They also possess venomous dorsal and pectoral spines and can be dangerous if not handled properly. These spines can become a major issue once the saltwater catfish reach their mature size–up to 12 inches.

Plotosus lineatus are impressive but poisonous.

Obligate sponge or coral feeders

Even supposedly easy-to-feed fish species can sometimes turn their keepers' hair gray by refusing to accept standard aquarium foods. But when a fish requires a very specific food item in its diet that is difficult or impossible for the average aquarist to provide, the likelihood of that fish surviving for long in captivity is minimal. For example, certain large

Ornate butterfly fish, *Chaetodon ornatissimus.*

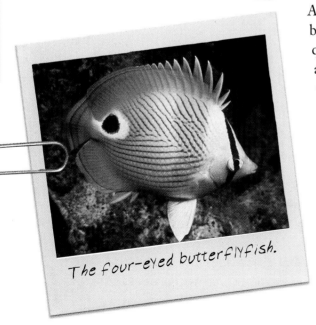

The four-eyed butterflyfish.

pomacanthid angelfish, including among others the conspicuous angelfish (*Chaetodontoplus conspicillatus*), the rock beauty (*Holacanthus tricolor*), and the blue-striped angelfish (*Chaetodontoplus septentrionalis*), feed primarily on coral polyps or sponges. Even if they eventually learn to accept standard aquarium fare in captivity, they generally will not thrive on it. I should add that there are now frozen foods on the market that are specifically formulated to meet the dietary needs of obligate sponge feeders, but even these may not be adequate for extremely finicky angels.

Their rigid dietary requirements aside, most large pomacanthid angelfish are unsuitable for the beginner aquarium because they are extremely demanding when it comes to water quality and will often become ill and/or go on a "hunger strike" when water conditions begin to deteriorate.

As a general rule, what's good for the angels is good for the butterflies. That is, many of the same dietary and water quality concerns that apply to pomacanthid angelfish also apply to the closely related butterflyfish (family Chaetodontidae). While some butterflyfish can be kept successfully by advanced aquarists, most are poorly suited for the beginner's tank. Certain species, including the four-eyed butterflyfish (*Chaetodon capistratus*), the ornate butterflyfish (*Chaetodon ornatissimus*), the chevron butterflyfish (*Chaetodon trifascialis*), and several others, will fare poorly under even the most experienced aquarist's care. With so many similarly colored and patterned butterflyfish on the market, many dealers can't identify the different species with 100-percent accuracy, let alone provide their customers with accurate dietary information for each species offered for sale. Rather than condemn a beautiful specimen to an untimely end in captivity, it's better to pass on the angelfish and butterflyfish for your first marine aquarium.

Fish needing a constant supply of tiny live foods

Much like the seastars, seahorses (family Syngnathidae) are considered by many to be true emblems of the sea. For this reason, along with their unique body shape and fascinating reproductive behavior, marine aquarists are often tempted to keep seahorses in their aquariums. Unfortunately, they seldom live long in captivity unless their keepers go to great lengths to satisfy their specialized dietary needs and their demand for superior water quality.

Chaetodon paucifasciatus.

Take one look at the tiny, tube-shaped mouths of these animals, and you can tell right away that they're highly specialized feeders. Seahorses, along with the other syngnathids, the pipefish and seadragons, require an almost constant supply of very tiny live food items, such as marine rotifers, daphnia, and newly hatched brine shrimp. Standard offerings of flake, frozen, and freeze-dried foods a couple times a day simply will not suffice. Three to four (or even more) small feedings of live food a day would be more in line with what these fish require. Considering how hectic most of our schedules are these days, finding the time to provide four or more feedings a day seems highly unlikely–not to mention the impracticality of maintaining a steady supply of the live food items they need.

Fish that don't ship well

Unless you're fortunate enough to live on an island in the tropical Pacific (or you only buy tank-raised specimens), the marine fish you buy for your aquarium are likely to have traveled a considerable distance in less-than-ideal water conditions prior to arriving in your dealer's tanks. Many species are hardy enough to survive this prolonged shipping period with no ill effects. Others, such as the Moorish idol (*Zanclus cornutus*), are notoriously difficult to ship and rarely survive long in captivity. Even public aquariums have a hard time keeping these fish alive for long.

Chaetodontoplus conspicillatus.

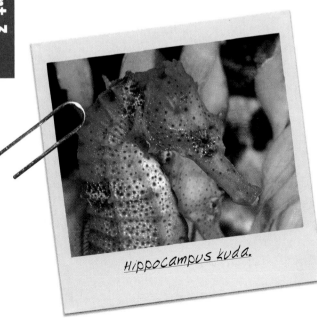

Hippocampus kuda.

The problem is, even though the Moorish idol tends to fare poorly in the aquarium, it is still prized by many aquarists for its exotic beauty and the characteristic long, flowing filament extending from its dorsal fin. Some find the Moorish idol so irresistibly beautiful that they will continue to buy specimens regardless of the outcome. And as long as a demand exists for these fish, collectors will continue to collect them, and dealers will continue to offer them for sale.

Sharks and morays: the "tank busters"

It's the rare marine aquarist who hasn't, at one time or another, contemplated keeping a shark. There's just something about these top predators that seems to epitomize the mystery and wonder of the ocean, and the temptation to own one can sometimes prove irresistible. The only trouble is, the odds rarely favor a shark's survival in the home aquarium. One obvious drawback is their ultimate size. Even some of the smaller bottom-dwelling species reach mature lengths that are way beyond the capacity of the average home aquarium. For example, the commonly sold gray bamboo shark (*Chiloscyllium griseum*) can reach a length of up to 30 inches. Try fitting that in our "model" 55-gallon (209-liter) aquarium! The popular peppered catshark (*Galeus piperatus*) is far more diminutive but still reaches the respectable length of 1 foot–no great white, perhaps, but still pretty large as aquarium specimens go.

Along with reaching "tank-busting" proportions, sharks are surprisingly sensitive to poor water quality and cannot tolerate high nitrate levels. Also, sharks are extremely sensitive to even the mildest electrical signals in their environment and can be driven to distraction by the stray voltages that sometimes are

Part 3

The poor man's Moorish idol

If you're really taken with the exotic beauty of the Moorish idol and feel you simply can't live without one, consider purchasing a bannerfish (Heniochus acuminatus) instead. The bannerfish (a.k.a., the poor man's Moorish idol) is almost identical in body shape and coloration to the Moorish idol and has the same graceful, flowing dorsal filament. The difference is, the bannerfish is much hardier and more likely to adapt to conditions in captivity.

Heniochus acuminatus, the poor man's Moorish idol.

produced by electronic filtration and heating devices. In addition, most of the commonly sold shark species prefer cooler water with a high dissolved-oxygen content, which is quite different from the conditions favored by most tropical marine fish.

Perhaps the biggest problem with keeping sharks is their tendency to "hunger strike" when stressed. While some shark species will sample just about anything they can sink their teeth into in the wild, the combined stresses of capture, transportation, and re-acclimation to the home aquarium can put them off food permanently, even when all other conditions and water parameters are in the ideal range.

Another sharp-toothed, tank-busting predator that often stirs the imagination of marine aquarists is the moray eel. Actually, there are numerous marine eel species that are commonly known as morays, most of which get way too large for the average beginner's aquarium. To illustrate how large some morays can get, consider one green moray (*Gymnothorax funebris*) that I observed once while diving in the Florida Keys. As a general rule, morays only extend about one-third of their body length out of their dens during daylight hours (at night, they emerge completely and swim around in search of prey). Taking mask magnification into consideration, the moray in question easily had 3 feet of its body exposed (with a "neck" resembling a linebacker's), suggesting that another 6 feet

Part 3

That's a moray!

of its body remained hidden in the den. That's a whopping 9 feet of eel!

Granted, many of the species that are frequently sold to aquarists don't grow that large, but even "small morays," like the snowflake moray (*Echidna nebulosa*) and the leopard moray (*Gymnothorax undulatus*) can reach lengths upwards of 3 feet and 5 feet respectively. Along with reaching gargantuan proportions, morays are terrific escape artists and can wriggle their mucus-coated bodies through amazingly small gaps in the aquarium cover. Of course, when an escape goes undetected, the moray usually meets a dusty demise on the fish-room floor.

Unlike sharks, moray eels are generally good eaters in captivity and can be enticed with a broad variety of foods. However, since they're very non-discriminating when it comes to diet, they'll be more than happy to devour any tankmates small enough to fit into their mouths. Morays also have very poor eyesight and may confuse an aquarist's hand with their favorite natural prey item, the octopus. When this occurs, the result for the unwary aquarist can be a painful, infectious bite. Since their dagger-like teeth angle backward to prevent seized prey items from escaping, it can be very difficult, once bitten, to break free of the moray's bite.

Are There Good Sessile Invertebrates for Beginners?

It's safe to say that many of the corals and other sessile invertebrates sought after by reef aquarists are highly sensitive when it comes to water quality and the spectrum and intensity of their lighting. However, there are some invertebrates that are slightly more forgiving when it comes to aquarium parameters, hence making them more suitable for an aquarist's first foray into the realm of the mini-reef. This is not to say that any sessile inverts will thrive under wildly fluctuating water and lighting conditions. They won't. I'm merely suggesting that you'll be more likely to enjoy success with your first mini-reef aquarium if you choose from hardier stock to begin with.

So, which invertebrates are best for beginners? To

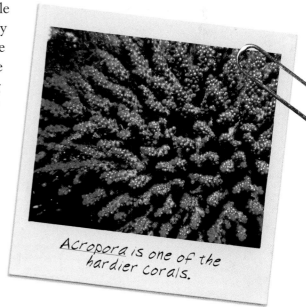

Acropora is one of the hardier corals.

Acropora nobilis.

Monastraea cavernosa.

keep things simple, we'll focus our attention on some good choices from three tried-and-true groups, including (in no particular order) the soft corals, the polyps, and the mushroom polyps. The animals in these groups (along with the hard corals, sea anemones, and jellyfish) all belong to the cnidaria phylum. All cnidarians have a similar radially symmetrical body plan with a central mouth/anus surrounded by numerous tentacles that are armed with harpoon-like stinging cells called nematocysts. But, as you'll see, there are quite a few variations on this one simple theme.

These corals are a bunch of softies!

At this point, it might be helpful to explain the difference between soft and hard corals because these watered-down descriptors don't really give you much to go on. Simply put, all hard corals (also called stony corals or true corals) manufacture calcium carbonate skeletons, whereas soft corals do not. Soft corals do have calcium carbonate in their tissues, but it is in the form of tiny spicules (called sclerites) rather than a large skeleton. You can also distinguish soft and hard corals from one another by the number of tentacles on each polyp. Soft corals have them in multiples of eight, while hard corals have six or more, but never eight. Another distinguishing trait of many (but not all) soft corals is the presence of small side branches (called pinnules) on the tentacles, which give the polyps a feathery appearance.

It is the hard corals, especially small-polyped varieties like the various species of *Acropora* (the elkhorn and staghorn corals) and *Montastrea* (the mountainous star corals), which are actually responsible for building tropical coral reefs. When hard corals die, their skeletons are left behind and serve as a foundation for

Part 3

other coral colonies. Over thousands of years, coral skeletons are continually deposited on top of one another, causing the reef to grow in turn. With few exceptions, hard corals are too touchy when it comes to water quality and lighting for the novice reef aquarist, so you're better off "getting your feet wet" with soft corals first.

The leather corals (*Sarcophyton spp.*) are some of the best soft corals for the novice reef aquarist. In the wild, these animals will thrive under less-than-perfect conditions that prohibit the growth of hard corals. Leather corals come in two distinct forms. Some species are mushroom-like in appearance, with a stalk that supports a polyp-covered disk. Other species have a more prostrate, encrusting habit, with an abundance of tiny polyps emerging from a broad, flattened base. These corals get their common name from the color (usually brown, beige, or yellow) and leathery texture exhibited by the main body mass when the polyps are withdrawn.

Don't be surprised if the polyps of a newly introduced leather coral remain withdrawn for several days. This is a natural response to changing conditions, not an indication of poor health. The polyps will re-emerge after having a chance to acclimate to the conditions in your aquarium. If given excellent water conditions, leather corals will grow rapidly in the aquarium and can even be propagated by taking cuttings and attaching them to pieces of live rock.

Lobophytum and *Sinularia* soft corals are very similar to the *Sarcophyton* leather corals in growth habit and appearance. *Lobophytum* corals are usually encrusting

Yellow leather coral, Sarcophyton elegans.

Toadstool leather coral.

Part 3

types, while *Sinularia* species are either encrusting, tree-like, or something in-between. Their colors range from pink to purple to beige. Species from both genera are very easy to maintain, even for the beginner.

The pulse corals of the *Anthelia* and *Xenia* genera are also excellent choices for the beginner's mini-reef. These corals are so named because of the continuous pulsating movements that are exhibited by the polyps of certain species. Ironically, only a small number of these so-called pulse corals actually pulsate in this manner. Nonetheless, they are very beautiful and relatively easy to maintain. Pulse corals come in shades of beige, brown, white, and even purple. In some species, crowns of flower-like polyps are borne atop long, slender stalks. Other species spread horizontally along the substrate by means of runners (called stolons) with feathery polyps emerging along the length of each runner.

Like the leather corals, pulse corals will spread quickly, colonizing neighboring rocks, if provided with excellent water conditions. Just be aware that the encrusting pulse coral varieties can be somewhat invasive and may inhibit the proper development of neighboring invertebrates. Fortunately, simply cutting back the offending coral or moving the affected animal to a different location in the aquarium will quickly reverse any adverse effects.

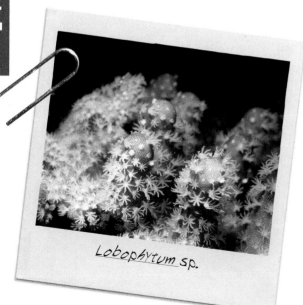

Lobophytum sp.

The star polyps (*Clavularia* and *Cornularia* spp.) are another group of soft corals well suited to the beginner's reef tank. Like the encrusting pulse coral species, these corals spread by means of horizontal runners, with polyps occurring along their length. Under optimal aquarium conditions, star polyps will grow rapidly, spreading out to adjacent solid substrates (i.e., the rockwork) with their runners. Of particular interest are the green star polyps, or starburst soft corals (*Clavularia viridis*). These extremely hardy corals have pale green polyps with bright green centers that are strikingly beautiful when fully expanded.

A passel of perfect polyps

Some of the easiest sessile invertebrates to maintain in captivity are the various zoanthid polyps (a.k.a., the coral

Part 3

polyps or the sea mats). While not true corals, zoanthids exhibit many of the same fascinating characteristics, making them equally desirable to beginners and advanced reef aquarists alike. Most species of these anemone-like polyps are truly colonial. That is, groups of polyps are attached by their bases to a single encrusting membrane, through which they share nutrients and nervous impulses. They get their common name, sea mats, from their propensity to form enormous mat-like colonies on the coral reefs. In the wild, many zoanthid species thrive in very shallow waters and may even be exposed during periods of low tide, making them highly adaptable to changes in temperature and salinity.

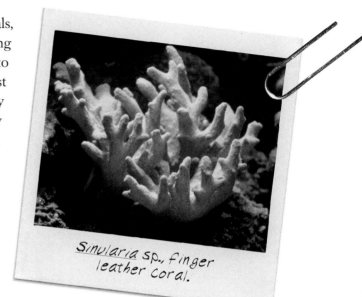

Sinularia sp., finger leather coral.

In terms of body plan, zoanthid polyps are very reminiscent of true anemones, possessing a button-shaped oral disc that is surrounded with two rings of tentacles and attached to a stalk. The only difference is, true anemones tend to be more plump and robust in appearance. Zoanthids come in a wide range of colors, including different shades of brown, dark green, lemon yellow, and turquoise. Most species are relatively small, reaching a maximum size of approximately one inch (2.54 centimeters) in diameter.

In a well-maintained aquarium, zoanthids will spread prolifically (as their common name implies) either by budding from the base of an individual polyp or by sending out runners. In spite of the fact that they reproduce "like rabbits," zoanthids generally will not attack neighboring invertebrates and, at the same time, seldom elicit aggression from other species. Of notable exception are the encrusting anthelia pulse corals, which have been known to sting zoanthids.

Zoanthids seem to thrive in areas of high water turbulence, so be sure to provide ample water movement in your mini-reef with a few strategically placed powerheads or filter returns. The only weakness to these relatively "bulletproof" invertebrates is that they can be smothered by heavy growths of filamentous algae. Deep-water species such as *Parazoanthus axinellae* (one of the non-colonial species) seem to be especially sensitive to

Part 3

Xenia sp.

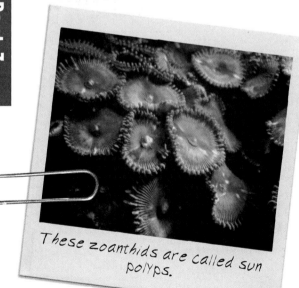

These zoanthids are called sun polyps.

algae overgrowth. To minimize this problem, it's important to keep the dissolved nutrient level in the aquarium low with a high quality protein skimmer and through regular partial water changes. It may also help to cut back slightly on the amount of time the lights are turned on each day.

One of the most commonly available species is *Zoanthus sociatus*, which is frequently sold under the name green polyps or green sea mat. These polyps are bright green overall, with yellowish-green at the center and on the margins of their oral discs. Other justifiably popular species that you may come across include, *Zoanthus danae, Parazoanthus gracilis, Parazoanthus swiftii, Palythoa caribaeorum*, and *Palythoa tuberculosa*. And that's just scratching the surface!

Make room for mushrooms!

The mushroom polyps (order Corallimorpharia) have been a mini-reef mainstay for many years and, like the zoanthid polyps, are supremely suited for the novice reef aquarist. As you've probably already guessed, their common name is derived from the mushroom-like shape of the individual polyps. Each animal consists of a flattened oral disc, which closely resembles a mushroom cap, attached to a short stalk. The stalk expands or contracts depending on the amount of available light. In a well-lit aquarium, the oral disc is almost flush with the substrate, but when lighting is more subdued, the stalk stretches out to bring the animal closer to the source. On some species, the oral disc is covered with very short tentacles, while tentacles are absent altogether on others.

Like the zoanthid polyps, mushroom polyps are often sold in "colonies" on pieces of rock. However, they are not colonial in the true sense of the word. Several individual polyps may

aggregate together in one small area, but there is no integration of tissue or sharing of nutrients. On the contrary, the base of each polyp is attached directly to the substrate. Mushroom polyps are more diverse in size and coloration compared to zoanthids. In size, they range from approximately one inch (2.54 centimeters) in diameter up to a whopping 12 inches (30 centimeters), and they come in various shades of brown, beige, red, blue, and green. Some even sport variously colored stripes, blotches, or spots.

Under excellent aquarium conditions, mushroom polyps will reproduce with abandon. This is achieved either by budding from the base or by the division of a single polyp into two separate, distinct polyps. The only drawback to their prolific reproductive habits is that, whereas zoanthids are non-aggressive with their tankmates, mushroom polyps pack a powerful sting and won't hesitate to use it on neighboring invertebrates. Surprisingly enough, however, they don't tend to show this aggression to zoanthid species.

Mushroom polyps also differ from zoanthids in that they don't seem to do as well in turbulent water conditions. When positioning them in the tank, try to find calmer areas with minimal water flow. If necessary, you can always rearrange the rockwork or redirect a powerhead in order to create such an area.

So which mushroom polyp species are best suited for the beginner's mini-reef? Actually, that's a question easier asked than answered. Most of the specimens offered for sale come from one of four genera: *Actinodiscus*, *Rhodactis*, *Discosoma*, or *Ricordea*. The problem is, it is often difficult

Actinodiscus coeruleus.

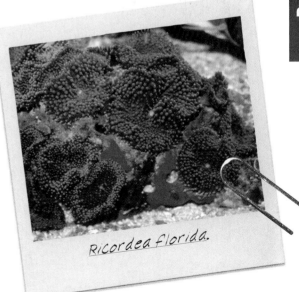

Ricordea florida.

Part 3

Wonderful Worms

Soft corals and polyps aren't the only easy-to-keep sessile invertebrates. The tubeworms (a.k.a., feather duster worms) are also well-suited for life in the beginner's mini-reef. One of the biggest advantages of these animals, apart from their beauty, is that they don't require any specialized lighting.

Tubeworms of interest to aquarists fall into one of two categories, the sabellid worms and the serpulid worms. Sabellids encase their bodies in soft parchment-like tubes, revealing only their large, feathery feeding tentacles. The serpulid worms, on the other hand, produce small stony tubes and have much shorter, often conical, feeding tentacles that come in various shades of red, yellow, blue, black, or white. The tentacles of each are rapidly withdrawn at the approach of a perceived threat.

Tubeworms are filter feeders and will thrive on newly hatched brine shrimp, marine rotifers, or commercial liquid invertebrate foods. Take care when selecting tankmates, however, as many fish and crustaceans include tubeworms as a regular part of their daily diets.

to tell the different species apart with any degree of certainty, even for the experts. So it's highly unlikely that your dealer will be able to provide more than the generic name for any given specimen–if he even knows that much. But don't be too concerned about species identification. As long as you select healthy looking specimens and provide excellent water quality and lighting, you'll get superior results with your mushroom polyps.

16

Sessile Invertebrates for Advanced Reefkeepers

In the last chapter, I suggested that it's a good idea to start out with some of the hardier sessile invertebrates, such as soft corals and polyps, when stocking your first mini-reef aquarium. Well, eventually, your invertebrate husbandry skills and your confidence level are going to build to the point where you're ready, willing, and able to experiment with some of the more sensitive invertebrates. You'll master the subtle art of maintaining impeccable water quality, and you'll learn how to keep all of your critical water parameters, including (among others) the temperature, pH, specific gravity, nitrate level, and calcium concentration, in the optimal range. You can be proud of yourself at this juncture; you've reached a very significant milestone in the marine aquarium hobby!

Bubble Coral, *Plerogyra sinuosa*

Euphyllia divisa, frogspawn coral.

Step up to stony corals

With few exceptions, reef aquarists eventually want to keep at least one or two stony coral specimens. Since "stonies" largely rely on the photosynthetic zooxanthellae residing in their tissues for survival, they are extremely sensitive to lighting, even more so than the soft corals and polyps we discussed in the previous chapter (many of which are also photosynthetic, I might add). Excellent water quality is also of the utmost importance. These conditions being met, there are certain species among the large-polyp stony corals (LPS corals) that will do quite well under the care of a slightly more advanced reefkeeper. Most small-polyp stony corals (SPS corals), on the other hand, are really only suitable for expert reef aquarists.

One of the best stony corals for reef aquarists to "cut their teeth on" is the bubble coral (*Plerogyra sinuosa*). During daylight hours, this aptly named coral looks very much like a mass of translucent velvety-white or fawn-colored bubbles. At night, the bubbles deflate slightly, revealing the polyp mouths and numerous stinging tentacles that it uses to capture plankton and to keep other invertebrates from encroaching on its territory. Give this fast-growing coral, and all the other corals in your mini-reef for that matter, ample room to expand to its full dimensions and to prevent stinging injury to its neighbors. You may need to observe its nighttime behavior to get an idea of how far its tentacles can reach.

For the most part, bubble corals can derive all the nutrients they need from their symbiotic zooxanthellae, but occasional (weekly or biweekly) offerings of chopped fish, shrimp, or krill, nestled gently between the bubbles will help keep these corals in superior health.

Trachyphyllia geoffroyi, open brain coral.

Another good choice for a first stony coral is the frogspawn coral (*Euphyllia divisa*). This animal has a very prominent, almost tree-like skeleton and thick, semi-transparent tentacles tipped with solid white dots–for all intents and purposes, looking like a mass of frog eggs (hence the common name). Take care when situating this coral, as it can expand its soft tissues to surprising dimensions. *E. divisa* is also very aggressive and can inflict a powerful sting. In addition, it possesses so-called sweeper tentacles that can extend well beyond the range of the feeding tentacles to sting competitors.

Like the bubble corals, frogspawn corals are photosynthetic and can get by with little or no supplemental feeding. If you do choose to feed this species, place small portions of krill or finely chopped fish among the tentacles. As a point of interest, in contrast to most large-polyp stony corals, frogspawn corals feed primarily during the day and retract their feeding tentacles at night.

The last LPS coral I'd like to discuss (although there are many other species worth trying that we won't get into here), the open brain coral (*Trachyphyllia geoffroyi*), is certainly not the least when it comes to beauty. In fact, this coral sports almost surreal coloration, ranging from fluorescent green, pink, or purple to deep crimson. Its meandering soft tissues, which are delightfully convoluted and covered with numerous narrow ridges, emerge from a conical skeleton. Open brain corals do not firmly attach themselves to reefs. In the wild, the pointed end of the skeleton is typically buried in a sandy substrate. To keep from being buried in sediment, the animal can inflate its soft tissues with water to raise itself up out of the sand.

Tridacna crocea.

This ability to inflate the soft tissues also allows open brain corals, as well as many other LPS corals, to maximize their surface area, thereby maximizing the amount of light that reaches their photosynthetic zooxanthellae. It also helps to eliminate any detritus that may settle on the animals in their sandy natural

Part 3

habitat. At night, the soft tissues deflate, and short feeding tentacles emerge to capture plankton. Unlike the bubble corals and frogspawn corals, open brain corals are relatively slow growing and do not have the propensity, nor the capacity, to aggressively attack and sting neighboring invertebrates.

As with the other two corals we've discussed, open brain corals can get all of their nutrition from zooxanthellae. Supplemental feedings should be limited to occasional offerings of finely chopped meaty foods.

Beautiful bivalves: the tridacnid clams

The high-intensity lighting and pristine water conditions favored by stony corals are also required for the proper maintenance of a completely unrelated yet equally stunning group of invertebrates, the tridacnid clams (better known as giant clams). Like many corals and anemones, these beautiful bivalves have symbiotic zooxanthellae in their tissues, more specifically, in their fleshy mantles, that produce all of the nutrients the clams need to survive. With tridacnid clams, the brightly colored mantles are the most attractive feature, although the deeply fluted shells of some species add interest as well. The brilliant mantles, which get their color from specialized pigment cells called iridophores, come in shades of blue, green, purple, gold, and various combinations thereof, depending on the particular species. There may also be considerable color variation from individual to individual within a given species.

Since the mantle typically faces upward toward the light source, tridacnid clams are best viewed from above, which means they should be placed lower in the aquarium for the most pleasing esthetic effect. In tanks over 18 inches tall, this may make it necessary to utilize metal halide lamps in order for an adequate amount of light to reach the clams. Full-spectrum

Tridacna derasa.

Filter-feeding flame scallop.

Part 3

fluorescent tubes or compact fluorescents will suffice for shorter tanks.

Most of the so-called giant clams belong to the *Tridacna* genus, and there is considerable diversity among the species when it comes to growth rate and ultimate size. To give you an idea of the potential size differential at maturity, consider that the smallest and most widely available species, *T. crocea*, reaches only nine inches in length. *T. maxima*, another species that is commonly available to aquarists, grows to approximately one foot. Moving up in size, we have *T. derasa*, maxing out at around 20 inches. Then we get to the biggest of the bunch, *T. gigas*, the definitive "giant clam," which can achieve an astounding 3 feet across!

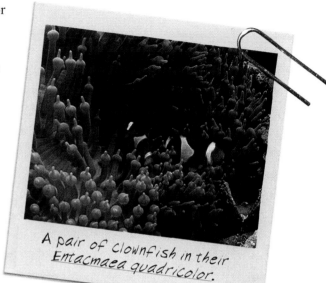

A pair of clownfish in their *Entacmaea quadricolor*.

In order to maintain their ponderous shells, tridacnid clams will extract a considerable amount of calcium from the aquarium water. For this reason, it's very important to supplement routinely with calcium in order to maintain a constant level of around 450 mg/l. Otherwise these clams will never reach their true potential. Strontium and iodine are also important elements for tridacnid clams. The former promotes shell

Filter-feeding flames

The tridacnid clams aren't the only beautiful bivalves suitable for the reef tank. Another animal that is well worth the effort it requires is the flame scallop (*Lima scabra*). This remarkable Caribbean species has an attractive scarlet-colored mantle that is fringed with numerous bright red tentacles. Other, almost identical species can be found on reefs throughout the tropics.

Flame scallops technically are not sessile invertebrates, as they are capable of "swimming" by clapping their shells together to escape predators or to move to a more satisfactory location. Once they settle on a spot, however, they will affix themselves to the reef with thread-like holdfasts.

Unlike their tridacnid cousins, flame scallops are not photosynthetic and rely exclusively on filter feeding to survive. And they have rather hearty appetites. In the aquarium, they will thrive on frequent offerings of baby brine shrimp, marine rotifers, or commercial invertebrate food. Take care when choosing motile invertebrates and fish to include with *L. scabra* because some (i.e., seastars and triggerfish) will be more than happy to make a meal of them.

Part 3

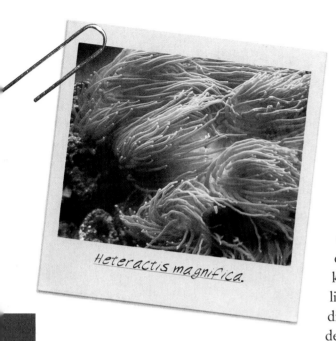

Heteractis magnifica.

development, while the latter is used for the production of their iridophore pigments.

Sea anemones

The sea anemones are another group of sessile invertebrates that almost all reef aquarists aspire to keep at one time or another. However, in your quest for suitable anemones to add to your mini-reef, don't be surprised when you hear or read completely contradictory accounts of how difficult anemones are to keep alive in captivity. Some sources will tell you that they are extremely hardy and easy to keep; others will claim that anemones are almost certain to die in the confines of the aquarium and that keeping them is tantamount to murder. The truth, of course, lies somewhere in between. Some species are notoriously difficult to maintain, while others are seemingly impossible to destroy (remember the dreaded aiptasia from the chapter on live rock?). The key to success with anemones is familiarizing yourself with all of the requirements of a given species–and making sure that you can satisfy them–before buying it.

Most anemones have the typical cnidarian body plan–that is, a mouth surrounded by stinging tentacles atop a stout, fleshy base. Sort of like coral polyps on steroids! Unlike corals, anemones do not permanently affix themselves to the substrate and can detach their basal discs to move about in search of more suitable surroundings (or to wage war on neighboring invertebrates) if necessary. Their colors are highly variable depending on the species and the location from which they are collected, and they range in size from little more than a few inches in diameter up to approximately 3 feet across.

In common with many corals and the tridacnid clams, many anemones have symbiotic zooxanthellae residing in their tissues and, so, require a well-lit environment. To a certain degree, you can determine which anemones are "light hungry" and which are not by their color. As a general rule, species that exhibit dull white, tan, or brown coloration do not harbor zooxanthellae and can be kept under more subdued lighting. Brightly colored anemones, on the other hand, typically do harbor zooxanthellae and require full-spectrum, high-intensity lighting. Of course, this rule has its exceptions. For example, some anemones from temperate waters are very brightly colored but cannot tolerate intense lighting. Your best bet is to research any specimens fully before making assumptions about their light requirements based on coloration.

Of course, the thing that attracts most aquarists to sea anemones is their symbiotic relationship with clownfish. There's just something fascinating about seeing these delicate-looking fish nestled–seemingly without a care in the world–amongst the deadly tentacles of their host anemones. But in order to enjoy this spectacle, you'll have to select anemones that are natural hosts to different clownfish species. For the most part, these will be specimens from the Indo-Pacific region, which is the natural range of most clownfish.

For example, the sebae anemone (*Heteractis crispa*) and the malu anemone (*Heteractis malu*) are both natural hosts to a wide group of clownfish, including the sebae clownfish, the skunk clownfish, the tomato clownfish, and the maroon clownfish (*Amphiprion sebae*, *A. akallopisos*, *A. frenatus*, and *Premnas biaculeatus* respectively). These nearly identical anemones have cream-colored or slightly bluish bodies with purple- or pink-tipped tentacles.

Common clownfish and percula clownfish (*Amphiprion ocellaris* and *A. percula*) will feel right at home amidst the tentacles of the purple base anemone (*Heteractis magnifica*). This giant among anemones has a purple body with light brown tentacles tipped with yellowish green or a scarlet

Scarus psittacus, parrotfish.

Part 3

Sound asleep in a bed of mucus?

Many nocturnal predatory fish are quite adept at "sniffing out" and snatching diurnal fish as they lie sleeping in the various nooks, crannies, and crevices of the coral reef. But many parrotfish (family Scaridae) have evolved a very peculiar defense mechanism against these night-raiding piscivores—they shroud themselves in a cocoon of mucus before they fall asleep! The transparent mucus "pup tent" does not actually conceal the parrotfish visibly, but it does mask their scent, making them extremely difficult to detect in the blackness that engulfs the coral reef at night.

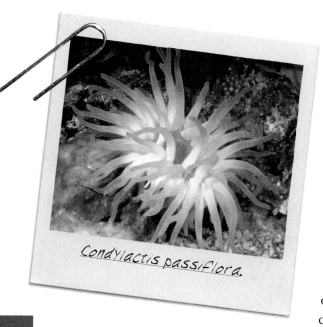

Condylactis passiflora.

body with pure white tentacles, depending on its origin. The only drawback to this species is that it can grow excessively large and, thus, requires a very large aquarium.

Another anemone known to host a wide variety of clownfish is *Entacmaea quadricolor*, which is called the bulb anemone because its tentacles bear a striking resemblance to baby bottle nipples. This species comes in various shades of brown, green, mauve, and even pink with green tentacles.

Of course, there's no requirement to keep anemones and clownfish together. The anemones will get along just fine in the aquarium in the absence of clownfish, and vice versa. However, it's interesting to note that clownfish will occasionally adopt other anemone-like invertebrates as hosts, including various corals and, surprisingly enough, even feather duster worms, when no suitable anemone is present in the aquarium.

As far as the level of difficulty is concerned, it seems the Indo-Pacific anemones that commonly host clownfish (and are generally the most beautiful) tend to be somewhat more challenging to maintain than species from the Caribbean or Atlantic, such as the Caribbean anemone (*Condylactis gigantea*) and the Florida pink tip anemone (*Condylactis passiflora*). I should also point out that it's a good idea to keep Indo-Pacific anemones and Atlantic anemones apart. Otherwise, constant territorial battling will ensue.

Part 3

A Mess of Motile Invertebrates

Regardless of the type of aquarium you decide to set up, you might want to liven things up a bit by adding a few motile (free-moving) invertebrates to your marine community. I'm talking about the various crustaceans, echinoderms, and gastropods that are routinely available to marine aquarists. Some of these organisms are ideally suited for inclusion in the fish-only system (Okay, technically it wouldn't be "fish-only" anymore, but let's not get hung up on semantics!), while others will fare better in the reef tank. Still others can be kept in either system with no problems. But remember, as with selecting any aquarium organism, it's important to research the needs and habits of any motile invertebrate before deciding to include it in your system so you can sidestep any compatibility problems.

Stenopus hispidus.

Lysmata amboinensis.

Periclimenes brevicarpalis.

A cocktail of super shrimp

Among the various shrimp that make their way into dealers' tanks, there are several species that are justifiably popular among aquarists due to their relative ease of maintenance, beauty, and fascinating behavior. The first species that comes to mind is the banded coral shrimp (*Stenopus hispidus*), also commonly called the boxer shrimp. This shrimp has a slightly transparent, white body disrupted by numerous red bands. It's long, arching, solid-white antennae sway gracefully in the current and make the shrimp seem much larger than it actually is. *S. hispidus* also wields absurdly oversized claws (also banded in red), which are typically longer than its three-inch (7.6 centimeter) body.

When first introduced to the aquarium, *S. hispidus* will be quite shy, spending the daylight hours hidden within the rockwork and emerging only at night to forage. However, as it gets more accustomed to its surroundings, it will overcome its initial shyness and spend much of its time in plain view. These shrimp can be quite aggressive toward conspecifics and should be kept one to an aquarium. An exception can be made in the case of mated pairs, which are often sold together. Feeding is easy for this species, as it will gladly accept just about any standard aquarium fare. *S. hispidus* will do equally well in both the fish-only tank (as long as crustacean-crunching species, such as triggerfish, aren't included) and the mini-reef.

The various cleaner shrimp of the *Lysmata* genus also make terrific aquarium inhabitants. These shrimp are so named because of their propensity to clean large, often predatory fish of parasites and dead tissue. Fish will even line up at coral reef "cleaning stations" for an

Part 3

opportunity to be picked clean by these shrimp and other cleaning organisms. In keeping with their nature, these shrimp will clean the fish in your aquarium and will even attempt to clean your hands if you allow them to. They're also relatively easy to feed, accepting most dry, freeze-dried, and frozen foods.

Perhaps the most popular, as well as most frequently sold, cleaner is *L. amboinensis*. This shrimp has a yellow body and a prominent red stripe overlain with a narrower white stripe running the entire length of its back. *L. amboinensis* has graceful, arching antennae, but it lacks the oversized claws of *S. hispidus*.

LYsmata wurdemanni

The peppermint shrimp (*L. wurdemanni*) is another cleaner worth keeping. It gets its name from its rather surreal red and white coloration, which is somewhat reminiscent of peppermint candies. This shrimp makes a great mini-reef inhabitant due to its propensity to devour the dreaded aiptasia anemones. However, whereas *L. amboinensis* tends to be fairly outgoing, *L. wurdemanni* spends much of its time in hiding, especially when kept with a lively community of fish.

Of all the cleaner shrimp, my personal favorite by far is the blood shrimp, or fire shrimp (*L. debelius*). This species has a blood-red body with pure white legs and antennae. A few small white dots appear along its back as well. This is an animal that must be seen to be believed. With its snow-white legs, it looks almost as if it's wearing white stockings, and its flowing antennae are perpetually in hypnotic motion. In my experience, *L. debelius* tends to be somewhat more delicate and sensitive (especially to excessively high water temperatures) than the other shrimp species we've discussed, but in terms of beauty, it beats the rest hands down.

Crabs with character

For the most part, "true crabs" get too large and rambunctious to make good aquarium inhabitants. However, certain crab species have become aquarium mainstays due to their generally peaceful deportment and fascinating (sometimes comical) behavior. Among

Part 3

these are the arrow crab, the Sally Lightfoot crab, certain hermit crabs, and the so-called anemone crabs.

As you might guess, the arrow crab (*Stenorhyncus seticornis*) is so named because of its arrowhead-shaped body. This crab gets around on exceedingly long and spindly legs (up to six inches or 15 centimeters), giving it a rather spider-like aspect. (Note: those with arachnophobic tendencies might find this crab's appearance somewhat startling.) But whatever you might think of its looks, the arrow crab is generally well behaved in both fish-only and mini-reef aquariums. The only desirable invertebrates this crab will torment include other arrow crabs, which it will fight to the death, and possibly tubeworms. To the delight of many reef aquarists, they've also been known to devour carnivorous bristleworms, a common plague of the mini-reef.

Stenorhynchus seticornis

The little Sally Lightfoot crab (*Percnon gibbesi*) is another excellent choice. More genuinely crab-like in appearance, the Sally Lightfoot may be a better option than the arrow crab for arachnophobes. This crab is typically a drab greenish brown in coloration, but what it lacks in color, it certainly makes up for in character. Its two front claws are in perpetual motion, continually plucking algae and food scraps from the rockwork and placing them in its mouth, looking very much like a greedy little child with a plate of French fries. It also has two tiny appendages, one over each eye, which continually flick up and down in comical fashion. Due to its herbivorous tendencies, the Sally Lightfoot crab makes an excellent addition to either the fish-only tank or the mini-reef.

Hermit crabs are widely available at a very reasonable price to hobbyists, and many species make terrific additions to the marine aquarium. As most people know, hermit crabs are born without a shell to protect their elongated bodies and so must borrow (or steal) the shells of other invertebrates–usually univalve mollusks. In the aquarium, as in nature, hermits are part of the "cleanup crew," as they routinely scavenge uneaten food items and will heartily consume nuisance algae.

Care must be taken when selecting hermit crabs because they range considerably in size and disposition in the aquarium. Some of the larger species can be very destructive to sessile invertebrates as they roam around the tank in search of food. Smaller species such as *Calcinus tibicen*, *Phimochirus operculatus*, and *Paguristes cadenati* are generally better choices, especially for inclusion in a mini-reef. *P. cadenati*, the scarlet hermit crab, with its bright red legs and distinctive yellow face, is, perhaps, the most commonly sold of the three. The drawback to this species (among others) is that it is largely nocturnal and may remain hidden in its shell during the day, although these crabs have been known to shift to a more diurnal lifestyle when that is the only time food is made available.

Perhaps the best crabs for the mini-reef are the anemone crabs, or porcelain crabs (*Neopetrolisthes* spp.). These little "gems," which often measure one inch (2.54 centimeters) or less across the carapace, look very much like miniature true crabs, although they differ in that their abdomens can unfold from beneath their bodies. They are also filter feeders, using feathery projections on their mouthparts to trap tiny particulate matter, whereas true crabs tend to scavenge or hunt for their food. Like clownfish, anemone crabs make their home among the stinging tentacles of anemones and often occupy the same anemone species favored by clownfish in the wild. They can be kept in the aquarium without a host anemone, but they don't tend to fare as well, and you won't be able to enjoy their fascinating symbiotic behavior.

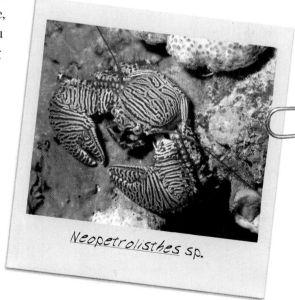

Neopetrolisthes sp.

These crabs come by their other common name, porcelain crabs, honestly. Their bodies are typically white overall with variously colored spots, depending on the species, giving them the appearance of fine painted porcelain. For example, the popular *N. ohshimai* has reddish brown spots in irregular patterns across its carapace, claws, and the bases of its legs. *N. alobatus* has dark brown or blue dots, while *N. maculatus* has a dense covering of chocolate-colored spots.

Excellent echinoderms

Among the invertebrates known as echinoderms, there are several animals worth keeping in a marine aquarium, including certain seastars, brittlestars, sea urchins, and sea cucumbers. Another major group of echinoderms, the crinoids (or feather stars), tends to fare poorly in the aquarium. These animals are best left to live out their fascinating lives on the natural coral reefs. Echinoderms (members of the Echinodermata phylum) are characterized by a pentamerous radially symmetrical body plan (the body can be divided into five parts around an axis), spiny skin, the presence of tube feet (tiny appendages that aid in locomotion, predation, and respiration), a simple internal skeleton made up of calcite crystals, and a unique water vascular system. However, as with the cnidarians, there are ample variations on this simple theme from one group of echinoderms to the next.

Star power

The seastars (or starfish, as most of us once knew them) are probably the most widely recognized of the echinoderms. Most seastars have five arms, radiating out from a central disc, but some have more. The crown-of-thorns star, which has gained notoriety in recent years for the devastating impact it has had on coral populations, has upwards of 23 arms at a time. Most seastars have amazing regenerative abilities. That is, they have the capacity to re-grow limbs lost to predation or some other injury. In fact, a seastar can survive as long as the central disc and part of one limb are left intact.

Brittlestar.

> ### Molt-induced panic
>
> If you decide to include crustaceans in your aquarium, be aware that all crustaceans molt. That is, they shed their rigid exoskeletons as a normal part of the growing process. Immediately after molting, a crustacean is extremely vulnerable to predation and will go into hiding for a couple of days while its new, soft exoskeleton hardens off. While this is a completely normal occurrence, it can lead to panic when an inexperienced aquarist finds the animal's molted exoskeleton (which, at first glance, looks very much like a complete animal) and, seeing no evidence of the living crustacean, assumes it has died.
>
> I should add that certain crustaceans occasionally have difficulty molting (possibly due to iodine deficiency) and may even lose their lives in the process, but this usually isn't a problem in a well-maintained aquarium with correct and stable water parameters.

Part 3

seastars feed primarily on other invertebrates or detritus, depending on the species. Those that actively hunt invertebrates tend to favor clams, scallops, and other bivalves, worms, and fellow echinoderms. The way in which a seastar devours a bivalve is really quite bizarre. First, it seizes the shell with its hydraulic tube feet. Then, it pries the two halves of the shell apart and actually extrudes its stomach into the shell. At that point, the seastar secretes a digestive enzyme onto the soft parts of the bivalve, which breaks down the tissues and makes them easier to consume.

In the aquarium, offerings of chopped fish, clam, scallop, shrimp, and large particulate foods are adequate. However, as seastars require excellent water quality and very low nitrate levels, care must be taken to avoid overfeeding and polluting the water. Most seastar species will get along well with a community of fish, but specimens for the mini-reef must be chosen with care. Otherwise, many of your prized invertebrates may be served up as costly entrees.

A good rule of thumb when selecting seastars for the mini-reef is to leave out specimens that have knobby backs, such as the common knobbed seastar (*Pentaceraster mammillatus*) and the red-knobbed seastar (*Protoreaster lincki*). Knobbed species tend to be omnivorous and so cannot be trusted around valued sessile invertebrates. On the other hand, smooth-skinned detritus feeders, such as the blue seastar (*Linckia laevigata*), and small, inoffensive species, such as the red seastar (*Fromia elegans*) and the orange seastar (*Fromia monilis*), will do quite well in the mini-reef.

This is the featherduster, *Sabellastarte magnifica.*

Protoreaster lincki.

Part 3

Neopetrolisthes sp.

Paguristes cadenati.

Brittlestars

With the brittlestars, we get into another group of invertebrates that are best left out of the arachnophobe's aquarium. Most brittlestars are shy and retiring filter feeders or scavengers, but some species are efficient predators and will rush out of hiding with alarming speed to grab food–much too spiderlike for some tastes. However, for the rest of us, brittlestars are a great option. They are especially useful in the mini-reef, where they earn their keep by scavenging uneaten food items from hard-to-reach places. They are also inoffensive to corals and other sessile invertebrates as they roam about in search of food.

Like the seastars, brittlestars have five limbs, but they are generally longer in relation to the size of the central disc, more slender, and more flexible. Some species have pronounced spines along the length of each arm, while others have smooth, almost serpent-like arms. Their limbs also have the tendency to break off easily if these animals are handled aggressively, which accounts for their common name. A lost or damaged limb is no cause for concern, however, since brittlestars will quickly regenerate any lost appendages. Most brittlestars are fairly subdued in coloration, but red or orange specimens are sometimes offered for sale.

Brittlestars of interest to the marine aquarist include, among others, the Caribbean sponge brittlestar (*Ophiothrix suensonii*), the giant red brittlestar (*Ophiocoma wendti*), and the banded brittlestar (*Ophioderma brevispinum*). Each will do quite well in the confines of the aquarium under the same high-quality water conditions favored by seastars.

Part 3

The spiniest echinoderms

At first glance, you'd never make the connection between sea urchins and their seastar cousins, but the two are closely related. These "pincushions of the sea" are typically spherical in shape with numerous spines covering their bodies. Anyone who has ever had the misfortune of treading upon a sea urchin while wading in shallow water will likely never forget the experience. Protruding between the spines are tube feet and pincerlike organs called pedicellariae that are used to clean the animals and to defend against predation.

Echinometra lucunter.

Sea urchin species feed in one of several ways. Some are purely herbivorous and graze on algae, while others scavenge dead animals and detritus. Some species are actually solution feeders, which means they absorb the nutrients they need to survive directly from the water. All require excellent water conditions and will waste away rapidly if conditions begin to deteriorate. Promptly remove any urchin specimen from the aquarium if its spines begin to droop or shed. This is a sure sign that the animal is in poor health and will likely die, and a decomposing sea urchin can really wreak havoc on your aquarium's water quality.

Urchins with long, needle-like spines, such as the long-spined urchin (*Diadema antillarum*) and the blue-spotted urchin (*Astropyga radiata*), should be handled with extreme care, since their spines can easily puncture the skin. Also, they can do considerable damage, albeit unintentionally, to the tissues of soft corals, anemones, and large-polyp stony corals, so take care when choosing their tankmates. Better choices are short-spined species, such as the pencil urchin (*Eucidaris tribuloides*) and the rock-boring urchin (*Echinometra lucunter*). The common urchin (*Echinometra mathaei*) is also well suited to aquarium life, but it can inflict a painful sting if handled improperly.

Of cucumbers and apples

The last group of echinoderms we'll look at is the sea cucumbers. With this group, the kinship with the seastar is even more difficult to discern, but all of the necessary

Part 3

Pseudocolochirus
sp.

echinoderm traits are present. For all intents and purposes, most sea cucumbers look like stretched-out sea urchins with the spines removed. Obviously, one could also argue that they look like shriveled terrestrial cucumbers (sea pickles?).

Like the sea urchins, sea cucumbers feed in different ways depending on the species. Some, such as the black cucumber (*Stichopus chloronotus*), sift through the substrate, swallowing gravel, digesting detritus, and ejecting any indigestible material from their rear ends. Others are filter feeders that capture plankton from the water with the tentacles (actually modified tube feet) surrounding their mouths. The filter feeding species can be very difficult to maintain in captivity, as they require several daily feedings of live brine shrimp or rotifers to survive.

One significant characteristic of sea cucumbers that aquarists should consider before buying a specimen is their propensity to discharge their viscera into the aquarium when disturbed. This sticky, threadlike substance can entangle fish and other

Greedy little apples

In spite of the inherent challenges, one filter-feeding sea cucumber–the strikingly beautiful sea apple (*Pseudocolochirus axiologus*)–is very popular with reef aquarists. This animal has a grayish-pink ovate body with pink, orange, or yellow tubefeet. It usually orients itself in an upright position, so its scarlet-colored, feathery feeding tentacles can capture plankton suspended in the water column. Its feeding behavior is a rather comical sight to behold, as it greedily thrusts each tentacle into its waiting mouth.

In common with most echinoderms, sea apples require outstanding water quality and will not last long in a poorly maintained system. But their unique beauty and amusing behavior more than justify the extra effort required to keep them in good health.

Part 3

marine organisms with fatal consequences. Some species, when agitated, will even exude a toxic substance into the water that is capable of killing everything in the aquarium. Not all species will do this, however, so it's important to "do your homework" on a given species before deciding to take it home.

Algae-grazing gastropods

Most marine aquarium dealers offer a varied assortment of snails at a fairly reasonable price, primarily for the purpose of algae control in the aquarium, and some species really earn their keep in this manner. Certain species also possess very beautiful shells, which make them doubly attractive. While there are literally thousands of gastropods inhabiting the world's oceans, we'll limit our discussion to a few commonly sold, herbivorous kinds that are safe for inclusion in both fish-only and mini-reef systems.

Astraea sp.

Turbo-charged snails

Marine snails of the *Turbo* genus are some of the best choices when it comes to algae control. These snails feed almost exclusively on undesirable film and filamentous algae, and one or two large specimens can literally strip an aquarium's rockwork clean of algae within a few days. Turbo snails typically have top-shaped shells with only a few whorls that are often encrusted with coralline algae. This tends to camouflage them perfectly against the backdrop of the aquarium's rockwork, making them difficult to discern without close inspection. *Turbo fluctuosus*, with its green to orange coloration, is both attractive and efficient and is well worth keeping. Snails of the *Astraea*, *Arene*, and *Cyclostrema* genera

Turbo snail.

Keyhole limpet, *Diodona* sp.

Calliostoma annulatum is best not used in a mini-reef.

are also good choices as they are close relatives of the Turbo snails and share their algae-munching propensities.

The limpets

The limpets (family Acmaeidae) are another group of marine gastropods that will rid an aquarium of irksome algae in short order. The shells of these snails lack whorls and have a low dome shape. They also vary considerably in color, pattern, and texture, depending on the species. Limpets are commonly found adhering to rocks in tidal pools. In the aquarium, they will exhibit this same behavior, seeking out protected areas within the rockwork. Since limpets are nocturnal feeders and tend to return to the same site after feeding each night, their keepers often wonder whether they are feeding at all. But such concerns are soon dispelled once the rocks are cleaned of algae.

The tops in algae control

Like the turbo snails, the so-called top shells have a (you guessed it!) top-shaped shell. However, they exhibit more spirals and a subtle iridescent sheen. *Tegula rugosa*, with its attractive checkered brown shell is one good option for algae control, as is *T. mariana*, which is smaller and has a mottled pattern on its shell. Top shells from the *Solariella*, *Margarites*, and *Lischkeia* genera are also excellent algae eaters. Members of the *Calliostoma* genus are best left out of the mini-reef. They will consume algae, but may also choose to sample certain sessile invertebrates.

Part Four
Care and Feeding

"Farmer Brown! Don't feed grass to my cowfish!"

Strapping on the Feedbag

Apart from maintaining impeccable water quality at all times, the most important role played by marine aquarists is providing the right types of foods in the right proportions to the fish and/or invertebrates in their care. This can be a challenge, considering the fact that most marine specimens are still wild-caught, and many of them have very specific dietary requirements that must be met if they are to adapt successfully to life in captivity. Simply put, providing proper nutrition can mean the difference between enjoying healthy and naturally long-lived specimens and continually having to replace deceased animals.

Not only is feeding important from a health and longevity standpoint, but it is also the only real

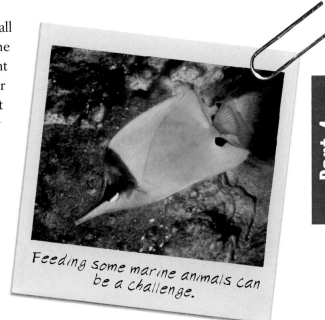

Feeding some marine animals can be a challenge.

Big aquarium fish, like this but-terflyfish, should have several small feedings a day.

Leafy greens are often given to marine fish; a better choice is marine algae.

opportunity we aquarists have to interact directly with our aquatic pets. The more "intelligent" fish species will soon recognize that their food always comes from one particular human and will reward him or her with almost puppy-like begging at mealtime. Some species may go so far as to feed directly from their owner's hand. This may seem insignificant in the grand scheme of things, but interacting with different aquatic species is one of the many rewards of keeping a marine aquarium.

Feeding our piscine pals

When it comes to feeding fish, variety is definitely the spice of life. The average community of tropical marine fish combines species with markedly different dietary requirements–some are primarily herbivorous, some are carnivorous, and others are omnivorous. Therefore, it's critical to offer an assortment of both meaty and plant-based foods in order to satisfy the different pallets of the fish in your aquarium, and considering the incredible diversity of flake, frozen, freeze-dried, fresh, and live foods available on the market today, it's never been easier to provide a varied selection of food items.

How much and how often?

As a general rule, fish should be fed no more than they can completely consume within a period of about five minutes. Any food left behind after that should be promptly removed with an aquarium net or vacuumed up with a siphon hose. Uneaten food that settles into the substrate or gets trapped in the rockwork will quickly decompose and degrade your water quality, so it's important to monitor the amount your fish are actually eating and make any necessary adjustments in the quantity you feed.

You'll also want to make sure that all the fish in the aquarium are getting enough to eat. It's not uncommon for larger, more aggressive fish to grab up all the food, depriving more passive species of sustenance, or for the mid-water feeders to gobble up the food before it reaches the bottom feeders. In other words, not only is it important that you familiarize yourself with the types of food a given species of fish will eat, but you should also be aware of its typical feeding behavior and the portion of the water column it tends to occupy.

So how often should you feed? Since reef fish are accustomed to browsing throughout the day, it's recommended that you offer multiple small feedings each day rather than one or two large feedings. Of course, once you factor in hectic work schedules and the various social commitments that most of us are bound by, two medium-sized feedings, one in the morning and one at night, might be more realistic. But whichever feeding schedule you adopt, keep in mind that you can do much more harm, both to the health of your fish and the quality of your water, by overfeeding than you can by underfeeding.

Foods for the herbivore

Fish that are primarily algae grazers in the wild, such as the tangs (or surgeonfish) and many angelfish, often suffer in captivity because they don't receive an adequate amount of plant-based food in their diet. Or if they are given plant material, it's usually in the form of terrestrial greens like spinach and romaine lettuce, which they can't digest properly. A better choice for tangs and other marine herbivores is marine algae. This can be provided in the form of dried green or red marine algae. Both of these products come in paper-thin sheets that can be cut into appropriately sized portions, depending on the number of grazers.

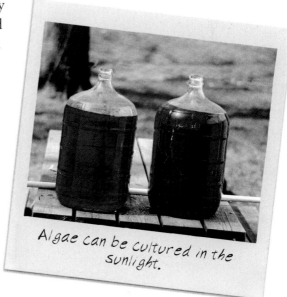

Algae can be cultured in the sunlight.

To feed dried algae, simply clamp a pre-cut section in a lettuce clip and place it on a rock in the aquarium, or secure the piece between the two sides of an algae magnet (with the aquarium glass in between) and slide the magnet down into the desired location. Remove and discard any

of bright eyes and bacteria

Bioluminescence (the emission of light by living organisms) plays an important role in the "after hours" coral reef community. One of the most dramatic examples of this is the flashlight fish from the Western Pacific. Flashlight fish possess special pouches filled with bioluminescent bacteria underneath each eye. When lit, these pouches serve to attract the tiny crustaceans that make up the flashlight fish's diet. These fish can also cover the bioluminescent pouch with a skin flap whenever they wish to extinguish the light. When a school of flashlight fish is kept in a dark aquarium, the aquarist will see only a group of white lights, flitting about the tank and blinking on and off at random.

The flashlight fish, *Anomalops katoptron.*

portions that are left uneaten after 24 hours, and replace them with fresh algae. Herbivorous fish prefer to graze continually throughout the day, so make sure an algae portion is always available in the tank.

Another way to provide algae to marine grazers is to place a glass container or a small aquarium filled with salt water in front of a window that receives full sun. Place a rock from your aquarium into the container, and wait for it to develop a nice shaggy coat of algae. Then, place the algae-encrusted rock back in the aquarium for your herbivores to graze, and put a different rock in the container to keep the process going. If you play your cards right, you'll always have a rock with a full complement of algae ready to replace the one that's been grazed.

Yet another way to satisfy the dietary needs of marine grazers is to feed them one of the frozen formula foods that are specially geared for herbivores. These formulas combine an assortment of marine algae, vegetable matter, and several types of seafood in one easy-to-feed product. I should add that there are similar frozen products on the market specifically formulated to meet the dietary needs of carnivores and omnivores as well.

Foods for the carnivore

The dietary requirements of meat-eating marine fish can be satisfied with any number of fresh, frozen, freeze-dried, and live foods. Suitable fresh foods include almost any seafood items you can buy from your local grocer, including fish (with the exception of oily species such as salmon, mackerel, and herring), shrimp, scallops, mussels, and clams. These items can be cut into bite-size portions for small- to medium-sized fish or served whole to larger predatory fish. If you buy fresh seafood in bulk quantities, you can store it in the freezer and thaw out small, manageable portions as needed.

Also, your aquarium dealer should have various frozen food items for sale, including brine shrimp, bloodworms, daphnia, and the above-mentioned formula foods, that are ideal for smaller carnivorous fish. These products will be either frozen in a slab, from which you can break off the desired amount, or in small easy-to-feed cubes. To feed any of these products, all you have to do is thaw a small portion in aquarium water and then offer it to your fish.

MYSIS shrimp.

Plankton, krill, brine shrimp, and bloodworms are some of the better freeze-dried foods for supplementing the diets of carnivorous marine fish. The freeze-drying process completely dehydrates these foods while retaining most of their essential nutrients. If properly stored (i.e., protected from moisture, heat, and light), freeze-dried foods have a relatively long shelf life compared to fresh and frozen foods. The only drawback to freeze-dried foods is that they can take a long time to rehydrate and so must be soaked for several minutes prior to feeding–not a problem if you have time to kill, but a bit of an obstacle when you're rushing off to work.

Several live foods are irresistible to carnivorous fish as well. Some of the better choices for small- to medium-sized fish are adult brine shrimp, bloodworms, and *Mysis* shrimp. Each will be accepted with gusto. Earthworms are another favorite if you can get them. The advantage to earthworms is that they come in all sizes, and you don't have to travel any farther than your garden to collect them. That is, of course, unless the ground is frozen solid. Since earthworms ingest large amounts of soil, be sure to rinse them thoroughly before feeding them to your fish. You can also store the worms in moist, shredded newspaper for a few days until the soil in their guts has been completely evacuated.

Larger predatory fish are often fed feeder fish (small goldfish, guppies, mollies, etc.) in captivity. This would seem like the most appropriate type of food to offer them, but,

Part 4

Daphnia.

Earthworms are easy!

One way to provide a year-round supply of earthworms for your carnivorous fish is to set up an earthworm compost bin in your basement or a heated garage. All it takes is a plywood bin (approximately 12"x16"x24") with a simple drainage grid at the bottom made of wooden strips, some suitable bedding material (chopped straw, shredded newspaper, etc), plenty of plant-based kitchen waste (carrots, lettuce, apples, coffee grounds, banana peels, and so on), and, of course, some earthworms (preferably red wigglers).

In a compost bin of this size, the worms will rapidly reproduce and eventually will be able to reduce as much as three pounds of kitchen waste per week. To keep the worm population in check, all you have to do is offer them to your fish occasionally. Not only do the worms make excellent fish fodder, but theyíll also reward you with their nutrient-rich castings that you can use as an organic slow-release fertilizer to feed your garden plants.

ironically, it isn't. Feeders are bred for only one purpose—to feed other fish. Little effort is made to keep them in good health or even to keep them fed, so they tend to be sorely lacking when it comes to nutritional value. Also, it has been shown that marine predators that are routinely offered nothing but freshwater feeder fish end up dying prematurely of liver disease. This is a common occurrence with lionfish, which are often difficult to wean off feeders. Every effort should be made to start lionfish and other large predators on frozen brown silversides, lancefish, or other marine-based meaty foods as soon as possible.

Foods for the omnivore

Although we discussed the various feeding options for herbivores and carnivores first, most tropical marine fish are technically omnivorous, which means they require both meaty and plant-based foods in their diet. Their needs are relatively easy to meet because most staple flake and pellet foods are formulated for omnivorous fish. However, that doesn't mean that a constant diet of nothing but flakes or pellets will keep these fish in optimal health. Just like obligate herbivores and carnivores, they prefer a varied diet and will be healthier, more active, and more colorful if given some alternatives.

Part 4

A good approach to feeding omnivores is to offer one or two feedings each day of flake or pellet food and one supplemental feeding of a meaty item like frozen brine shrimp, frozen bloodworms, freeze-dried plankton, or chopped fish. When available, you can also present them with some live foods. Try to alternate the supplemental foods you offer, so your fish won't get bored with their menu. It's even a good idea to offer different varieties of flake or pellet food to make sure your fish are getting all of their nutritional needs met. Remember, all prepared foods are not necessarily created equal when it comes to ingredients.

Since most reef fish are mid-water or bottom feeders, it's a good idea to swish your flake food around in a cup of aquarium water for a few seconds so it becomes saturated and will sink readily. Flakes floating at the surface are generally useless to the fish and will be skimmed off quickly into the wet/dry prefilter chamber if such a system is in use. If you prefer to feed pellets, buy the sinking kind, as floating pellets are equally useless to most marine fish.

Feeding sessile invertebrates

One of the most perplexing issues confronting both the beginner and experienced aquarist alike is determining the most appropriate way to feed sessile invertebrates in a mini-reef aquarium. Fish we understand. To a certain extent, they're very much like us in that they'll thrive if given two or three balanced meals a day. And when they're hungry, they'll generally let you know it through their body language. But the feeding habits of sessile invertebrates (especially the

Live feeder fish aren't the best choice for carnivores.

Bloodworms are not worms, but the larvae of a midge.

Part 4

photosynthetic species) are definitely beyond the realm of human experience, and if they exhibit any hunger cues, they're certainly not perceptible to people. So what's an invertebrate fancier to do? Once again, the key is research. It's very important to learn the natural feeding habits of any sessile invertebrate before attempting to keep it, let alone feed it.

Should you feed "light hungry" invertebrates?

"Light hungry" corals, anemones, and Tridacnid clams get all of the nutrition they need from the photosynthetic algae residing in their tissues and, so, require little or no supplemental feeding. Remember, the unique symbiotic relationship between these invertebrates and their zooxanthellae was an evolutionary response to living in very nutrient-poor water. While most photosynthetic invertebrates have the capacity to ensnare plankton with their stinging tentacles (or in the case of the tridacnid clams, the capacity to filter plankton from the water with their siphons), they don't necessarily depend on these chance feedings to sustain themselves.

Limit any food offerings to very small quantities of newly hatched brine shrimp, marine rotifers, or a commercial liquid invertebrate food. Or better yet, withhold feeding altogether, and wait to see how the animals respond. After all, any benefit these animals will derive from supplemental feeding will be undermined quickly if water conditions begin to deteriorate as a result of overfeeding.

Feeding non-photosynthetic filter feeders

In contrast to their "light hungry" neighbors, non-photosynthetic, filter-feeding invertebrates, including (among others) certain soft corals, sponges, anemones, feather duster worms, and flame scallops, depend upon regular feeding in the aquarium. A daily feeding of marine rotifers, newly hatched brine shrimp, or a liquid invertebrate food is more than adequate to sustain most filter feeders. When feeding, it's a good idea to shut off the aquarium's filtration system, so the tiny suspended organisms aren't filtered out before the invertebrates have a chance to capture them. One way to ensure that each animal gets enough food is to dispense it directly onto its feeding tentacles (or over its siphon) with a turkey baster. Again, err on the side of feeding too little, especially when feeding commercial liquid invertebrate foods, to avoid fouling the water.

You may have noticed that I listed anemones as filter feeders. Technically this is true, since they can trap small planktonic prey with their tentacles. However, certain species may benefit from occasional offerings of larger meaty foods, such as shrimp, strips of fish, or other seafood items. These can be placed directly into their tentacles with a pair of forceps or aquarium tongs.

Crustacean cuisine

Small crustaceans, such as the hermit crabs, banded coral shrimp, and cleaner shrimp, will generally fare quite well on the same cuisine offered to omnivorous fish, and in most cases, they'll be able to get by on the food items left over by the fish. However, this should not be taken as justification to overfeed. Most small crustaceans can subsist on very little food and will not fill the role of "aquarium vacuum cleaner." In other words, uneaten food can still accumulate on the substrate and in the rockwork, causing your water quality to "crash," even when several scavenging crustaceans are present.

No bones about it!

As a note of caution, whole bone-in fish (especially feeders) should not be fed to sea anemones. They will attempt to consume whole fish, but they are not capable of digesting the bones properly. The way they get around this is to regurgitate the bones in an unsightly blob of mucus, which can really foul the water in your aquarium. So whenever feeding fish to an anemone, be sure to use only small strips of filleted meat.

Of course, you don't want to go to the other extreme either, feeding such small portions to the fish that no morsels are ever left over for your crustaceans. Though considering the fact that most of us tend to overfeed rather than underfeed, I would suggest that this is a highly unrealistic scenario in the fish-only aquarium. In the nutrient-poor environment of the mini-reef, on the other hand, you may need to go the extra mile to ensure that your crustaceans are getting enough to eat. The best way to achieve this is by placing sinking food items in the same, easily reached location each day. And don't worry, it won't take your crab or shrimp long to figure out where to go for regular feedings. Remove any uneaten portions after about one hour so they don't have a chance to decompose and degrade your water quality.

Part 4

Aquarium Health Care and Maintenance

Though this chapter is dedicated primarily to disease and health care in the marine aquarium, it also includes a section on routine aquarium maintenance. This is because, for all intents and purposes, the two subjects are inextricably bound together. Marine fish typically become ill and die as a response to declining environmental conditions or fluctuating water parameters. These stressors have a tendency to inhibit the natural disease-fighting mechanisms of marine animals, making them more susceptible to infectious agents, including various bacteria, fungi, viruses, and parasites. Disease can also rear its ugly head when a specimen is consistently fed the wrong foods or is fed too much of the right foods.

Lateral line disease in a batfish.

Signs and symptoms of fish disease

As you observe the day-to-day behavior of your fish, be on the lookout for these common warning signs of disease (possible causes are included in parentheses):

- Scraping or rubbing on rocks, substrate, or decorations (parasitic infection)
- White or black spots/gold-brown dusting (external parasite infection)
- Frayed, or disintegrating fins (bacterial infection or mechanical injury)
- Body ulcers (bacterial or parasitic infection)
- Warty growths (viral infection, usually lymphocystis)
- Cloudy eyes (physical injury, bacterial infection, parasitic infection)
- Bulging eyes (bacterial, viral, or parasitic infection)
- Distended abdomen (overeating, internal bacterial infection, parasitic infection, tumor)
- Excessive secretion of body slime (protozoan parasitic infection, presence of ammonia, excessively high pH, presence of copper)
- Increased respiration (parasitic infection, low dissolved oxygen level, high water temperature, presence of ammonia)
- Long-term change in coloration (many diseases and water-quality problems can cause this)
- Refusal to eat (improper diet, aggression from tankmates, many infectious diseases)

Listlessness (most infectious diseases, low water temperature, poor water quality)

Marine ich.

Of course, in some instances, marine fish die as a result of the combined stresses of collection (including unethical collection practices, such as poisoning with sodium cyanide) and prolonged shipping, which in no way reflects on the skills or diligence of the aquarist. For example, if a fish dies shortly after purchase and testing reveals that all of the aquarium's water parameters are correct, you can usually assume that the fish was in poor condition when you purchased it. If you should experience this at some point, don't be discouraged because it happens to the best of us. Just be sure to inspect the next specimen thoroughly to verify that it looks healthy, eats well, and exhibits the appropriate coloration before buying.

Part 4

Don't forget the quarantine tank!

We've already discussed the importance of quarantining newly purchased specimens before releasing them into your main aquarium, but it's something that bears repeating. A quarantine tank will allow you to isolate and monitor new acquisitions for several weeks to determine whether they are harboring harmful pathogens or parasites that could infect the rest of the fish in your community, potentially causing the death of all your valued specimens. While quarantining fish is no absolute guarantee that dangerous microbes won't make their way into your aquarium, it will certainly decrease the odds. A quarantine tank will also make it possible to administer any necessary medications directly to a sick animal without having to subject your healthy specimens to a battery of caustic chemicals. When a fish that is kept in a mini-reef becomes ill and requires medication, a separate quarantine tank is essential because sessile invertebrates generally cannot tolerate the chemicals used to treat fish diseases.

Ectoparasites.

Bacterial infections

Pathogenic bacteria can always be found in aquarium water, but they tend to cause disease only when a fish's immune system has been suppressed due to some form of stress or physical trauma. Injury from rough handling or fighting, poor water quality, and inadequate nutrition are just some of the possible stressors that can predispose a fish to bacterial infection. Also, fish with pre-existing diseases will commonly contract secondary bacterial infections.

Bacterial infection.

Part 4

Fish may have more than one disease at the same time.

Bacterial infection can manifest itself either externally or internally. External infection typically is in the form of fin-and-tail rot or body ulcers. With fin-and-tail rot (as you might guess), the soft tissues and rays of the fins begin to deteriorate or take on a tattered appearance. It's easy to distinguish bacterial rot from mechanical injury–such as that caused by fighting–because rotting fins are typically red or brown in color at the margins. Body ulcers are red, swollen lesions that often start in one area then expand to other parts of the fish's body. Keep in mind that, if left unchecked, external infection can spread to the fish's internal organs and bloodstream, sometimes with fatal consequences.

The most troublesome internal bacterial infection experienced by marine fish is fish tuberculosis (not to be confused with the tuberculosis that affects humans), or wasting disease, which is caused by the *Mycobacterium marinum* bacterium. This disease usually affects older fish, especially those that are kept in overcrowded aquariums with inadequate filtration and generally poor water quality. Symptoms vary depending on the stage of the disease and the particular species of fish that is infected, though some of the more common signs include change in body color, emaciation, and bulging eyes.

The best way to treat bacterial infections is to take all necessary steps to prevent them from happening in the first place. This means using the best possible protein skimming and filtration equipment and adopting outstanding aquarium water management practices in general. Of course, the most important step you can take is to stay on top of those regular partial water changes.

There are proprietary medications and various antibiotics that can be used to treat bacterial infections after an outbreak occurs, but typically they are effective only when the disease is caught in the early stages. Always keep in mind that antibiotics should be used judiciously and in strict accordance with the manufacturer's recommendations. Administering an improper dose can have an adverse impact on your aquarium's biological

Part 4

filtration. Worse yet, if you fail to complete a full course of treatment, you may inadvertently be selecting for antibiotic-resistant strains of bacteria.

Fungal and viral infections

Fungal diseases are relatively uncommon in marine fish, but occasionally they do occur after an injury or a parasitic infection, especially when water conditions are poor. The spores of pathogenic fungi are always present in marine aquariums, and they are surprisingly resilient. When the spores begin to grow on an ailing fish's body, they send out numerous thin threads that actually penetrate deep into the tissues and organs of the fish. All that the aquarist can see at this point is a thin film or discoloration on the fish's body or gills.

Diagnosing a fungal infection is difficult, since the symptoms often mimic those presented by certain parasites. Proper identification is confounded even further by the fact that parasitic and fungal infections tend to occur together. As with preventing bacterial infection, the best way to deter secondary fungal infection is to improve the environmental conditions in the aquarium. However, if an outbreak should occur, treating the infected fish with malachite green, methylene blue, or one of the various proprietary fungicides will eradicate the problem successfully.

Cryptocaryon infestations can be quite severe.

Viral diseases are relatively uncommon among marine aquarium fish, though there is one–called lymphocystis–that you should be aware of. There is both good news and bad news concerning this disease. The good news is, it progresses very slowly and is rarely fatal. The bad new is, the disease is disfiguring, and there is no medication that will cure it.

Lymphocystis affects the fish's connective tissue, creating hard, warty growths on the trailing edges of the fins, on the body, and around the mouth. In severe cases, the growths that occur in the area of the mouth can prevent the fish from feeding properly, but normal

Part 4

behavior is unaffected otherwise. Unfortunately, the symptoms of lymphocystis can take so long to manifest themselves–up to ten days after infection–that all of the fish in an aquarium may be infected before the disease is detected.

Any fish exhibiting symptoms of lymphocystis should be removed promptly from the aquarium and placed in quarantine. While there are no drugs that you can use to treat the fish, it may rid itself of the virus after several months. Of course, you should monitor the rest of the fish in the community to determine if any have been infected, and no new fish should be added until you're certain that the aquarium is disease-free.

Parasitic infections: who sprinkled salt on my fish?

An aquatic Houdini

Octopuses make fascinating and extremely intelligent aquarium inhabitants. However, they are best suited for public aquariums or advanced hobbyists who are better equipped to meet their special needs. Octopuses are a challenge for the average aquarist for several reasons. For one thing, they demand exceptional water quality and a very stress-free environment. Octopuses tend to release ink (sepia) into the aquarium when under stress, thereby polluting their own water. Octopuses are also amazingly short-lived. In fact, most species (of an appropriate size for the aquarium) have a lifespan of little more than three years. But perhaps the greatest drawback to keeping octopuses in the aquarium is their incredible ability to escape through even the tiniest gap. Remember, an octopus can squeeze its entire body through any opening large enough to accommodate its parrot-like beak. Unfortunately, when this happens, the "aquatic Houdini" usually ends up drying out on the floor before the aquarist has a chance to detect the escape.

While fungal and viral diseases may be relatively uncommon, parasitic diseases are almost inevitable. If you keep tropical marine fish, you'll most likely, at one time or another, have to combat parasites. And there are lots of parasitic critters out there, including various protozoa, copepods, flukes, and worms. To keep things simple, we'll limit our discussion of parasites to the two that you are most likely to experience: marine velvet (*Amyloodinium ocellatum*) and white spot disease, or saltwater ich (*Cryptocaryon irritans*). Both are caused by protozoa with very similar life cycles and modus operandi, and both are introduced into the aquarium through infected (usually non-quarantined) fish.

With marine velvet, tiny parasitic protozoa attach themselves via a root-like structure to the body, fins, and gills of a host fish and live off its tissues. To the naked eye, the parasites look like a fine white- to gold-colored dust. Once they reach maturity, they detach and settle to the bottom of the aquarium, where they form cysts. Inside each cyst, cell division starts to take place, producing over 200 spores (called dinospores). Eventually, the cysts rupture, freeing the dinospores, which then swim off in search of a host fish to infect.

Part 4

Fish infected with marine velvet will express their discomfort by scraping their bodies against the rockwork and substrate. Other obvious signs of infection include pale coloration, excessive body slime production, and increased respiration. If not treated in a timely manner, marine velvet can cause the death of the infected specimen in short order.

Octopuses are fascinating, but not the best aquarium animals.

Saltwater ich is virtually identical to marine velvet when it comes to the life cycle of the associated protozoan. The physical symptoms of the disease are also very similar. The only difference is, saltwater ich is characterized by larger white spots instead of a dust-like coating. The white spots are actually cysts produced by the fish in an attempt to reduce the impact of the parasites. Like marine velvet, this disease will kill its host fish if not treated promptly.

Treating both of these parasites can be a challenge because most medications are only effective against the protozoa in the free-swimming and adult stages. The encysted parasites are unaffected. For this reason, it's necessary to maintain a therapeutic level of medication in the tank long enough for any cysts that remain on the substrate to release the free swimmers into the medicated water. This takes a minimum of 14 days for marine velvet and 21 days for white spot disease.

The most commonly recommended course of action for both marine velvet and white spot disease is to dose the water with a copper-based medication. If left in the system long enough, copper is very effective at eradicating these parasites. However, copper does have its drawbacks. For one thing, it is lethal in even minute concentrations to any invertebrates that aren't protected by a hard exoskeleton. For another, copper can be precipitated out of the water by various calcareous materials (e.g., the rockwork and substrate) and small amounts can be "dumped" back into the aquarium water for many years to come. This is no big concern in a fish-only aquarium, unless you intend to convert it to a mini-reef someday. If such is the case, you'll need to replace all of the rockwork and substrate before the aquarium can be considered safe for invertebrates.

Part 4

The freshwater dip

A good alternative to copper for treating marine velvet, white spot disease, and a host of other diseases is to give the infected fish a freshwater dip. This is a very simple procedure that is surprisingly effective, and if done correctly, your fish will experience minimal stress.

So how does fresh water kill parasites? Actually, it's a very simple process. Water tends to flow from areas of lower salt concentration toward areas of higher salt concentration. When a marine parasite (say, for example, the *Cryptocaryon irritans* protozoan) is placed in fresh water, the salt concentration is higher within the body of the parasite compared to the surrounding water. Therefore, water will flow rapidly into its body, causing it to burst from the osmotic shock–a fitting end for such an irksome pest, I think.

To perform a freshwater dip, fill a one-gallon glass or plastic container with fresh tap water. Remove the chlorine from the water with a liquid dechlorinating product, and make sure the temperature and pH are nearly identical between your main aquarium and the treatment water. Then, as carefully as possible, net the infected fish, and place it in the freshwater bath. Leave the fish in the bath for no more than ten minutes, and monitor it closely during the entire treatment. The fish may become disoriented at first and possibly lie flat on its side. This is a normal response and no reason for concern. However, if the fish begins to behave extremely erratically, you'll want to put it back in salt water as quickly as possible. After all, you don't want the cure to be worse than the disease.

A few words on using aquarium medications

If I had to sum up my feelings about aquarium medications in a single, succinct statement, I would have to say, "Don't use them unless it's absolutely necessary." Whenever possible, try to find an environmental solution to disease outbreak rather than a medicinal one. It's very difficult for the average aquarist to precisely diagnose the various ailments that can afflict fish without having access to a battery of laboratory equipment. And using the wrong drug to treat a disease or using the right drug incorrectly will only make matters worse for your fish.

If you decide that it is necessary to medicate the tank (as we've all done at one time or another), be sure to follow the drug manufacturer's dosing instructions to the letter, and try not to fall into the "if a little is good, more is better" trap. Also, keep in mind that you'll need to remove any activated carbon from your aquarium system before dosing the aquarium, as it will adsorb many dissolved medications from the water before they have a chance to do any good.

A schedule of aquarium chores

I've emphasized the importance of maintaining a stable environment in the marine aquarium repeatedly through the pages of this book. But, if you'll indulge me, I'll state it one more time and then shut my mouth about it (Did I just hear a collective sigh of relief?). The coral reef habitat is one of the most stable environments on earth, and the ultimate key to keeping reef organisms successfully in captivity is to approximate that stability as closely as possible in the aquarium. To achieve this, you'll need to commit yourself to a set schedule of routine aquarium maintenance chores. Following a set maintenance schedule will ensure that any problems are caught before they reach crisis proportions. In other word, you'll be more likely to notice them in the early stages when you'll still be able to correct them through small, incremental adjustments rather than through extreme measures.

The schedule I've outlined here is one that I at least try to adhere to. I'm presenting it to you as one possible option. Feel free to modify it as you see fit or as your particular circumstances dictate. You may find it helpful to write out your maintenance schedule in the form of a checklist so you can mark off each chore once it's been completed.

Daily duties
• Check the water temperature.

• Check specific gravity.

• Make sure all heating, filtration, protein skimming, and lighting equipment is functioning properly.

• Empty the accumulated waste from your protein skimmer collection cup.

• Clean "salt creep" from various aquarium surfaces.

• Top off fresh water lost to evaporation.

Part 4

• Check over your animals for signs of stress, injury, or disease (and, of course, to make sure none has died). This is best done at feeding time when the more skittish fish will emerge from hiding.

• Remove any uneaten food with a net or siphon.

Weekly duties
• Test for ammonia, nitrite, and nitrate.

• Check calcium level and add any necessary supplements or trace elements (mini-reef).

• Rinse off any prefilters to eliminate trapped "gunk" and uneaten food that could decompose and degrade your water quality.

• Scrape algae from the front pane of the aquarium.

Biweekly duties
• Perform, at the very minimum, a 10-percent water change (even better if done on a weekly basis). Gently vacuum the substrate to remove detritus.

• Remove and replace any mechanical filtration media. This should be done a few days before or after the water change to avoid disrupting the biological filter too greatly.

• Clean the cover glass. This is especially important in a mini-reef aquarium, since salt buildup, calcium deposits, and dirt on the glass can reduce the amount of light that reaches photosynthetic invertebrates.

• Check all of your power cables and electrical connections to verify that they are free of salt creep and in good condition.

Every six to eight weeks
• Replace airstones. They will undoubtedly be getting clogged, and therefore losing efficiency, after six weeks of use.

• Replace used-up carbon so it doesn't "dump" adsorbed pollutants back into the aquarium.

• Clean your protein skimmer and all filter housings, pumps, tubes, and hoses with aquarium brushes.

• Gently rinse your biological filtration medium/media in aquarium water.

Per manufacturer's recommendation
• Replace the fluorescent tubes or metal halide bulbs used to illuminate your mini-reef. This is usually recommended every six to nine months, depending on usage.

Staying With it
for the Long Haul

Now that you've taken the plunge into the fascinating realm of the marine aquarium, you'll soon discover that the rewards and challenges that lie ahead are almost limitless. Once you've mastered the basics and gotten that first critical taste of success, you'll be ready to expand your horizons to include the care of more sensitive and exotic species. And like almost every marine aquarist before you, you will eventually succumb to the temptation (or should I say compulsion?) to set up multiple aquariums to accommodate an ever-growing population of fish and/or invertebrates.

But getting the most out of the marine aquarium hobby is not completely automatic. It requires a

Be prepared for emergencies!

significant amount of effort and a willingness to learn on your part. The more effort you put into maintaining your aquarium and the more time you invest researching the characteristics and needs of various marine organisms, the more you'll succeed in your endeavors, and the more likely you'll be to stick with the hobby for the long haul.

So what steps can you take to keep your interest level high? For one thing, you can get connected to your local aquarium society, which will allow you to exchange ideas, information, equipment and even specimens with aquarists of all different skill levels. Also, there are numerous Internet chat rooms and message boards you can frequent to share your thoughts with fellow aquarists. I've found that this is an excellent way to get timely responses to healthcare issues and other problems I've encountered along the way. Of course, don't forget your trusted aquarium dealer. He or she can give you lots of friendly advice as well as keep you apprised of exciting new trends in the marine aquarium industry. In addition, you can continue to read every piece of marine aquarium literature that you can lay your hands on, including textbooks, magazines, newsletters, and journals. With the continued support of these influences, along with your own enthusiasm and ingenuity, you're sure to enjoy a lifetime of wonder and success in the marine aquarium hobby.

photographers

AquArt, Myles Aronowitz, Dr. H. R. Axelrod, Laurence Azoulay, Robert Bell, Cathy Church, Circona of America, Walter Deas, James Fatherree, Robert Fenner, U. Erich Friese, Bill Gately, Michael Gilroy, Robert Goemans, J. F. Hamel, Phillip Hunt, S. Johnson, Gary Lange, Oliver Lucanus, Ken Lucas, Ralph Mesa, Aaron Norman,John O'Malley, Mike Paletta, MP. & C. Piednoir-Aqua Press, Courtney Platt, Jose Reyes, Gunther Schmelzer, Dr. Ron Shimek, Mark Smith, Mary Sweeney, Dr. Z. Takacs, Edward Taylor, John Tyson, Maleta Walls, Robert Wederich, Katherine Wickstein, Matthew Wittenrich

Index